Mammals

An Artistic Approach

by
Desiree Hajny

Fox Chapel Publishing
Box 7948
Lancaster, Pennsylvania
17604

© 1994 by Fox Chapel Publishing

Publisher: Alan Giagnocavo
Project Editor: Ayleen Stellhorn

ISBN #1-56523-036-1

Photography: Cover - Bob Pollett, VMI Productions
               Photo Gallery - Bob Mischka
               Step by Step Sequences - Mike Hutmacher

Our thanks to the Pennsylvania Game Commission for their excellent reference photos. Also special thanks to Bob Mischka for his gorgeous photography found in the Photo Gallery chapter and to Keith Nisly of Discover Design and Communications (Lancaster , Pa.) for the design and production of many of the reference and carving charts contained herein.

Look in the back of this book for information on other patterns and resources available from the author.

To order your copy of this book,
please send check or money order for cover price plus $2.50 to:
Fox Chapel Book Orders
Box 7948
Lancaster, PA 17604-7948

Try your favorite book supplier first!

This book is dedicated
to my family and friends —
who believe in me.

Mammals: An Artistic Approach

Introduction

When I was approached to do a book on sculpting mammals from wood the first thing I did was to establish a set of objectives for the publication that I thought was appropriate for my style and, more importantly, for those interested in the book.

As the title implies, this is an "artistic approach" to carving. Something I wanted to avoid was doing a step-by-step method. I feel that this type of presentation limits the abilities of the person carving the particular project. My book is intended as a guide. It will allow you the flexibility to adapt certain ideas from the book that you may find relevant and combine them with your own unique style. As you progress through the book, keep in mind that experimentation and changing your projects to suit your needs will only enhance the final result.

In writing this book, I also wanted to include information on the animals to increase your knowledge on the subject, as well as foster an awareness of each animal's personality. This is an important part of carving, and one that is often overlooked.

Finally, my overall intention was to provide the reader with a resource that will improve his level of confidence in his carving abilities. This, in turn, will give him the opportunity to experiment more freely.

Desiree Hajny

Table of Contents

When Desiree Hajny picked up an X-acto® knife and a piece of wood in 1979, her intention wasn't to learn to carve mammals. All she wanted to do was show a group of high school students in Bassett, Nebraska, that art could be fun.

That task wasn't easy, she recalls. Bassett was a ranching community and many of its residents felt that art had no place in the schools. The students, too, were bored with the traditional approach to art.

"I had to find a way to show them that art is the basis of all that's man-made," remembers Desiree. "Cars, houses, roads... Everything starts with an idea and a drawing."

Then, one night while selling tickets at a basketball game, the idea to use woodcarving to teach art popped into her head.

"It was just far enough away from watercolors and drawings that I was sure it would grab their attention."

A local lumber yard donated wood and a car company in town saved lead from the inside of old tires to use in lead castings. Desiree learned along with her students how to draw up ideas, carve, texture and paint.

Desiree encouraged her students to work on whatever interested them. Some chose to carve sports items, some chose dragons, others chose letters. One student carved bits and pieces of a motor that fit together at the end of the year. And some, like Desiree, chose animals.

By the finish of the school year, her students had learned that art was a creative process, not something stiffled, and Desiree was hooked on carving.

Desiree wasn't able to focus fully on carving until six years later when she and her husband Bernie moved to Columbus, Nebraska, with their new son, Jeff. Jeff was 10 months old at the time and Desiree had decided to give up her career as a teacher and stay home with her son.

"I felt I was missing so much," she said. "I wanted to watch him grow. I wanted to see his first steps and hear his first words. I felt that if anyone was going to make mistakes raising him, it was going to be me."

With the support of her husband, they worked out a plan. Desiree would stay home with Jeff for a year and see if she could make enough money doing artwork to make ends meet. If things didn't work out, she'd go back to work full-time at the end of the year.

Desiree worked hard that first year to pick up any work she could find. She drew posters for local organizations, designed prints for T-shirts, and even did work for a printing company.

"All of a sudden the woodcarving took off," she remembers. "My pieces started to sell, and people were asking me to teach woodcarving classes."

Today, Desiree lives in Wichita, Kansas, and her carvings can be seen in private collections and at carving competitions and exhibitions nationwide. Her work has become so popular that several galleries in Colorado, Nebraska and Ohio now carry her work.

Desiree has never had any formal training in carving. In college at Peru State College in Nebraska she had hopes of becoming the first woman political cartoonist.

"I took all sorts of anatomy classes to know which parts of the human body to exaggerate," she recalls. "I sometimes find even now that the cartooning slips into my carving—especially when I want to emphasize a certain characteristic of an animal."

Because she's self-taught in carving, Desiree developed some "very strange techniques" in her early years. For example, she used a stippling technique to color in her cartoons and found herself using that same stippling technique to texture many of her early carvings. She has since relearned some of her techniques through watching and talking with other carvers.

"It did teach me an important lesson though," she says. "I know now that there's always more than one correct way to get something accomplished."

Many people in the carving community have high regards for Desiree and her work.

Ed Gallenstein, editor and publisher of *Chip Chats*, the bimonthly magazine of the National Wood Carvers Association, believes that Desiree is "easily one of the top-notch carvers in the country."

Peter Ortel, a caricature carver from New York, agrees. Desiree's carvings caught his eye at several shows because of their unbelievable likeness to the real thing.

"Desiree is the best at what she does," he says. "You look at one of her pieces, and your brain says, 'That's wood,' but your eyes say, 'No, that's fur.'"

Forward Roll
Woodcarvers Showcase-Silver Dollar City, Branson, MO
This piece and the next piece, "Dances With What?" showcase
Desiree's considerable talent in carving caricatures, although she is
better known for her highly realistic pieces.

Desiree modestly shrugs aside the glowing comments about her work and tells a story about her first big project.

"I wanted to give to my husband a coffee table as a wedding present. The top was decorated with five deer running through the woods. To show you what a green-horn I was... I picked walnut because it looked pretty. I had no idea it was such a hard wood. And I used an X-acto® knife to carve it. I finally gave it to Bernie two years after we were married."

In addition to traveling to competitions and exhibits, Desiree also travels across the country to teach woodcarving classes and give seminars to all levels of aspiring carvers. She finds teaching a real joy. Being a one-time high school teacher, she says that she was used to only a certain percentage of a class paying attention to her at any given time.

"In woodcarving classes everyone pays attention," she says. "I remember looking up during my first class and seeing everyone listenting. My jaw dropped. 'This is how teaching should be,' I thought to myself."

Larry Yudis, owner of The Woodcarving Shop, has sponsored several classes taught by Desiree. He believes that she is undoubtedly one of the most sought-after carving teachers in the realistic animal carving field.

"Her personality makes her a wonderful teacher," he says. "She instills an air of positive thinking in everyone in the class no matter what his skill level. She convinces people they're doing great with her air of enthusiasm."

Bob Micshka, a photographer who often shoots Desiree's pieces, notes that Desiree's influence on the carving field is becoming more and more obvious with every show.

"She's gotten so good that there's a whole genre of carvers who can be identified as her students by the look of their carvings," he says, "and this wouldn't happen if she weren't one of the best."

Along with the success of her carvings and her classes, Desiree has also branched out into other areas, including instructional videos and books. She has also been the subject of several magazine articles and local television shows.

Perhaps the biggest feather in her cap was the confirmation that she was chosen from a group of world-renowned artists to have her works reproduced by Converstion Concepts, Inc. of Fitchburg, MA. These limited edition wildlife reproductions are being marketed nationally and internationally.

Dances With What?
Second Place-International Carving Congress

Currently, Desiree and her family are in the middle of a move to a new house just inside the Wichita city limits. Her studio, now just a corner of an unfinished bedroom, will soon be a room finished just for her, with a dust collector, book cases and plenty of space for all her tools.

She likes to keep her studio filled with several in-progress projects at all times. While other artists need to be in the mood or inspired to create, Desiree wants to be able to work whenever she has the time—no matter what her mood. When she's in a good mood, she works on faces. If she's in a bad mood, she carves bases. And when she's in a creative mood, she focuses on drawing up ideas.

Among many other smaller projects, Desiree is now working on four major commissions. The first, just drawn on the wood and roughed out, is a sculpture of a fox family. The father fox is stretched out next to the mother who's playing with a cub. The second carving, still in the sketch phase, is of two wolves, one lying down, panting, and the other looking as if he's just heard a sound. The third, a coyote showing a mother, father and three pups, is still in the rough stage. The fourth, a panda with its baby, is a little further along. The entire sculpture is rough-carved, and the face of the mother panda is finished. Desiree's still not sure how to position the baby. She's debating whether it should look at the mother or off to the side.

"I make it a habit to always carve the head and face of a piece first," she says. "If the face doesn't reflect the piece's personality, I put it aside and start over. That way I don't waste valuable time carving the body, only to find out I don't like the face." She finds herself scrapping many carvings and starting over again until they have the right look.

Desiree uses both power tools and hand tools. She tries to experiment with as many different tools as she can because some tools have advantages that others can't give. She also wants to be familiar with a wide array of tools so that she is better prepared to teach her carving classes. "I don't want to limit my students to only what I know."

For beginning carvers, she has some serious advice. "Don't be afraid to listen to what people say," she says. "Don't be offended, because the good things they mean to say don't always come out that way."

Preparation for Battle
1st Place International Carving Congress

"Ask questions," is another piece of advice from Desiree. "Most carvers will be happy to answer questions and give you advice. They'll even take the time to tell you what tools they use and how they paint."

And finally, Desiree encourages people to, "Try different things. There's always another way to do something, and it's not always bad."

by Ayleen Stellhorn

Patience Worn Thin-1991
Dremel/DucksUnlimited Masters Carving Competition - Best of Show

Return to Yellowstone

Return to Yellowstone

Return to Yellowstone
Best of Show-Great Plains Woodcarving Show
1st Place-Woodcarvers Showcase, Branson, MO
A stunning piece capturing the attitude and poise of a wolf pack in the wild.

Peaceful Moment

Mystic Leaper

Regal Thirst-1989
1st Place-13th Canadian International Wood Carving Competition-Toronto
1992 Encyclopedia of Living Artists-entry piece

Winter Solitude

Winter Solitude

Sprucin
1991-Best of Show Grand Canyon State Woodcarvers 2nd Desert Festival
1991-Miniature Art Society of Florida-1st Place in Sculpture
1993-Chosen to be on a USA tour to represent miniature showpieces

Subtle Courtship
1st Place-1992-Design Source National Woodcarvers Showcase
1st Place-Great Plains Expo-Wichita - 1st-Group
1991-Calendar "Woodcarving Art"

Noble Curiosity

THE OTTER
River and Ocean Otters

Of all the mammals, the otter seems to offer endless possibilities for beautiful carvings. Its fluid lines, reminiscent of the "S-curves" so often discussed in sculpture, lend themselves to a variety of twisting and alluring poses. I'll provide a brief introduction to both the river otter and the ocean otter here, but you'll want to do further research at your local library, museum or zoo.

As its name suggests, the river otter lives in rivers, streams and lakes throughout much of the United States and Canada. Its stream-lined body is brown to grayish above; the chin and throat are grayish-white; and the underparts are a buff-color. Its tail is thick and round, tapers toward the tip, and moves in a back and forth motion when the animal is swimming. Its snout is broad and rounded, and its feet are webbed with long toes and sharp claws.

The river otter is a sociable animal. It is often seen frolicking about in the water, twisting and turning as it swims. The river otter is also fond of sliding down slippery, mud-covered or snow-covered banks near its home. Its playful personality easily translates into a fun and interesting carving.

The ocean otter, also as its name suggests, spends most of its time in the ocean waters off the west coast of the United States and Canada, coming ashore only during severe storms. Its fur is a glossy, dark grey above; its head and chest are buff-colored. Its flat tail moves in an up and down motion when the animal is swimming, and its feet are webbed and stubby.

The ocean otter lives in kelp beds along the rocky west coast shores where the shellfish it eats are common. It can often be seen backstroking in the water with its head held above the surface. The ocean otter brings the food it finds to the surface where it uses a flat rock balanced on its stomach to crack open tough shells. This posture, easily identified with the ocean otter, makes for a beautiful carving.

Planning to Carve an Otter

Once you have done some additional research and are comfortable with all aspects of the otter, it's time to plan your sculpture. One important thing to remember is that, like us, each otter will have its own personality and its own features. Some have longer noses, wider nose pads, wider set eyes or larger ears. Make your carving unique, but be careful not to go overboard. Don't make the ears larger than ever possible on a real otter, or set the eyes too far apart.

Think also about the overall impact of your piece. Everything about your otter will influence your carving. Is your otter an older or younger animal? Younger animals have smoother, sleeker coats; the coat of an older otter will be more ragged and faded. Is it winter or summer in your carving? Winter otters will have a thicker coat; summer otters will have a thinner coat. Is your otter well fed and plump? Or is he lean due to a rough winter with a scarce food supply? Is he angry, calm, or playful? His attitude will define his pose.

In this chapter, you'll find two different patterns for carving an otter—one pattern shows a swimming pose; the other shows a standing pose. Don't feel locked into these patterns. You can take the information presented here and change the pattern to suit your ideas. For example, say I want to carve a standing ocean otter instead of the swimming ocean otter shown in the pattern. All I need to do is copy the basic features of the swimming otter—his head shape, body shape, leg shape, etc.—and match them up with those of the standing otter. You can see the result on the standing ocean otter pattern in this chapter.

Knowing the otter's anatomy and how its body weight and muscles shift helped me to massage its body parts into their correct anatomical positions. I've also changed the swimming river otter to a standing river otter using this same method.

The new standing ocean otter can also be changed into a black-footed ferret, or an ermine, or a weasel. Just do a little research. Trace the new animal's features onto a piece of tracing paper. Next trace the standing ocean otter's outline. Adjust the pattern accordingly, and you have a new pattern from which to work.

Once again, I can't stress enough how important it is to really know the anatomical features of the animal you are planning to carve. Turning the standing ocean otter's head from the side to the front is not just a matter of carving the animal, cutting off the head, and turning its head to face front. Think of your own head and how the muscles in your neck change when you turn your head from the side to the front. The same muscle changes take place in the otter.

Carving Notes

If you are carving a standing otter, trace your full-sized pattern on to a 7" x 2" x 2" block of wood. The grain should run vertically.

If you are carving the swimming otter, trace the pattern on to a 2" x 8½" x 2½" block of wood. Make sure the grain is running horizontally.

If you have altered the pattern, make sure that you have left extra wood for shifts in the joints and balance, the curve of the spine, and other alterations.

Eye sockets are at a 65 degree angle from the centerline.

Use Drawings A and B to measure out the head.

Use Charts C through E to shape the face.

Use Chart F to carve the feet.

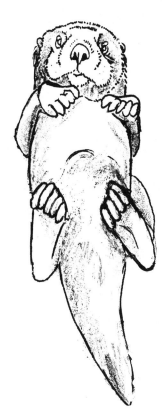

Swimming Ocean Otter

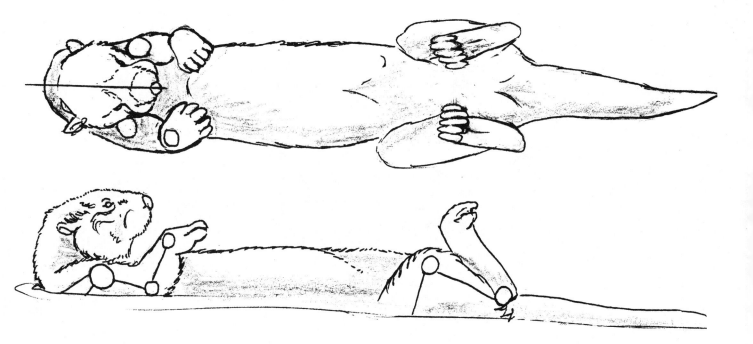

Standing River Otter

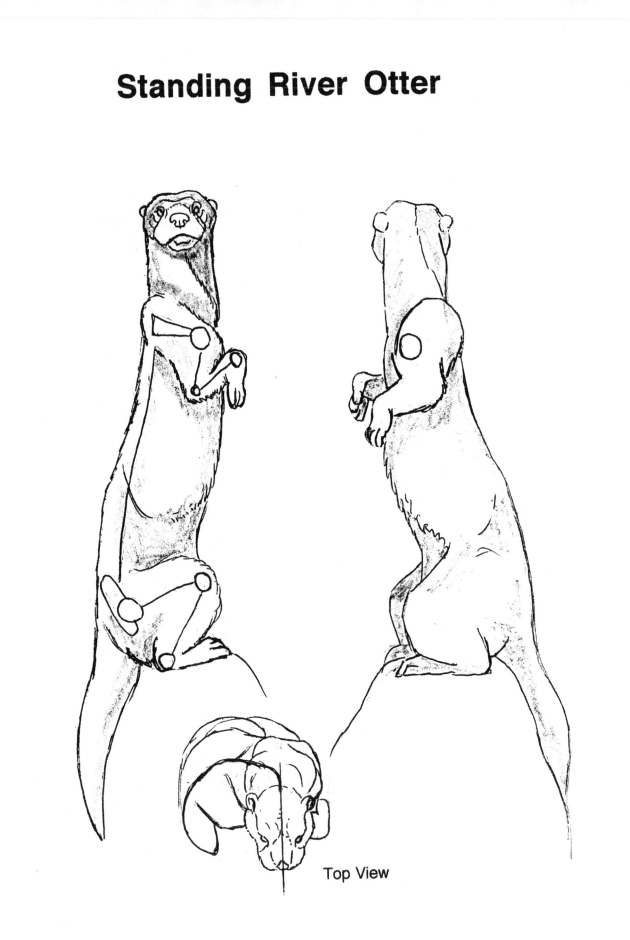

Top View

Standing Ocean Otter

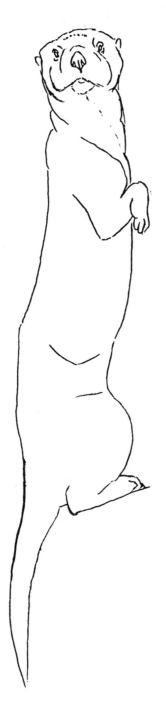

By incorporating the features of the
ocean otter into the standing river otter
pattern, I was able to create a new
pattern.

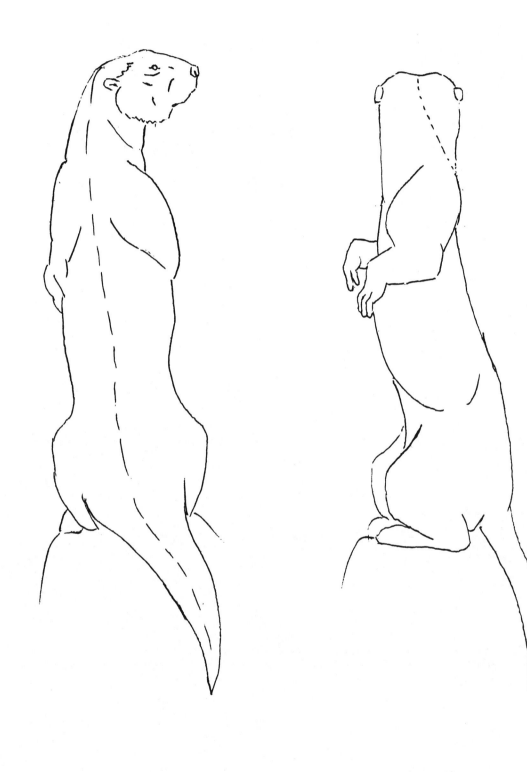

Swimming River Otter

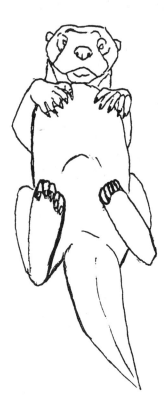

By incorporating the features of the river otter into the swimming ocean otter pattern, I was able to create an entirely different pattern.

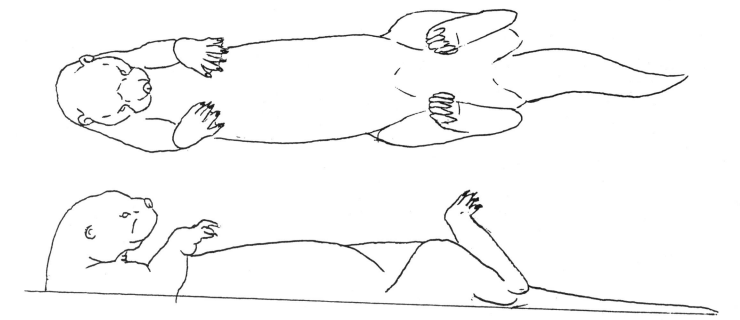

Black Footed Ferret

Tan body, blackish back bone, black
mask, whitish chin and muzzle. Black
feet and tip of tail.

Ermine

White body. Tip of tail and eyes, black.
Nose, pinkish.

Spotted Skunk

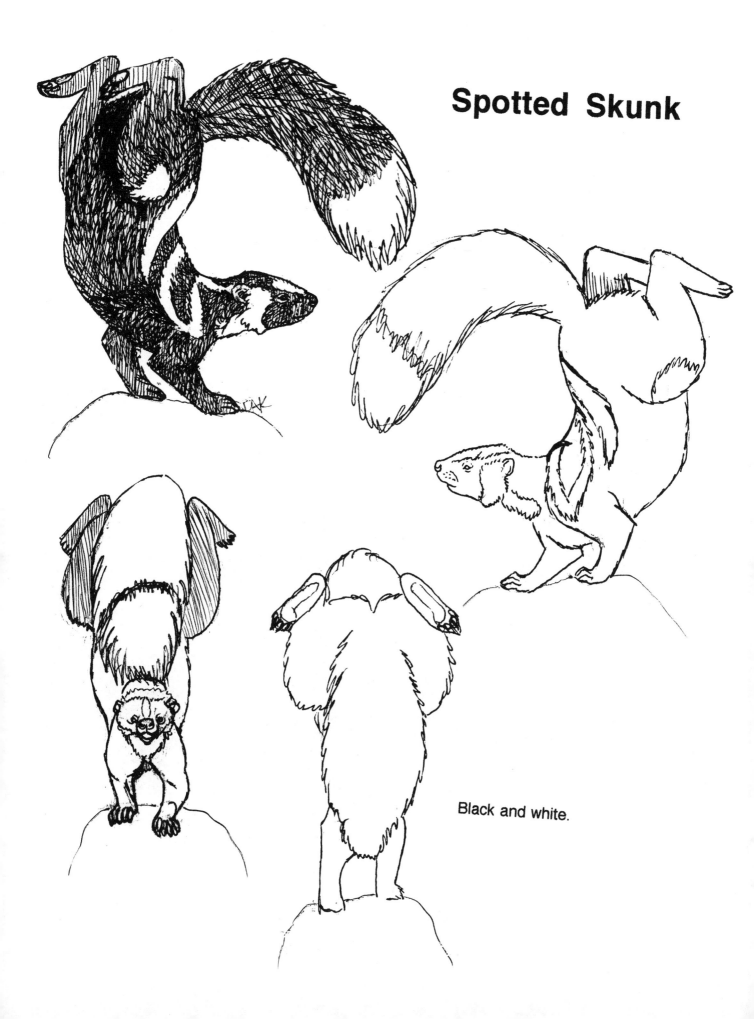

Black and white.

TECHNIQUES

Altering Your Pattern

Don't feel locked into using the patterns that are included here exactly as they appear. You can enlarge or reduce them with the help of a copy machine. I also include plenty of information to help you do some redesign—including simple changes such as turning the head and more complex changes such as altering the animal's pose. Use these instructions, found in each chapter, to mold these patterns to your own ideas.

Transferring Your Pattern

There are several ways to transfer a pattern to your block of wood. I will tell you how to use carbon paper, my choice, but you can also trace around a cut-out pattern with a pencil or a knife. Tracing the pattern onto acetate and attaching the acetate to the block is a third method.

To use carbon paper to transfer your pattern to the block of wood, simply place a piece of carbon paper, carbon side down, on the block. Place your pattern on top of the carbon paper. Using a pointed object, like a pen or pencil, trace along the lines of the pattern. When you remove the pattern and the carbon paper, the outline will appear on the wood. Repeat this process on the remaining sides and top of the block

Beginning to Carve

Remove excess wood until your rough has the curves and contours shown in the drawings and your own changes. Make sure after blocking in the shape to start on the face. When you get a good face established, a personality will emerge. Best of all the pressure is off—if you don't like the head, you haven't wasted valuable time on the body detail.

Draw a centerline from the top of skull down the bridge of the nose. If the design calls for a turned head, start the centerline from top of skull and pull the line in the direction of the turn. Measure from this line accordingly and remove any excess wood.

Measure out the distance between the edges of the nose pad from this centerline. It tapers up to the upper bridge. This area always goes up above the eye sockets. From the top view, the eye sockets angle outward from the center point. Leaving the bridge flat gouge out the socket area using a K#8 (4 mm) gouge or a ⅜" ball rotary bit.

Use any woodburner that has an adjustable thermostat to texture your carving. You'll find that there are many burner tips available on the market. I'll discuss the ones that I commonly use, but you'll want to experiment with others on your own.

I'll also cover some common burning techniques. But, here again, you'll want to experiment. The charts and drawings included in this section will give you a good starting reference.

The hair tract drawings for each animal show how to begin burning in the illusion of fur. Make sure you map out the direction of the fur first, considering the wind, gravity, and time of year in which your animal is being portrayed.

Begin by making small marks with the burner tip you've chosen to use. Be sure to layer these marks and cross them over each other once in a while, using a fluid motion. Animals don't have parallel hairs. The hairs on the face around the nose and the eyes are the shortest, so use any tip that comes to a point. Here, again, avoid putting in too many straight lines. Use a stab-pull motion.

To obtain shiny eyes, sear the wood of the eyeball with the side of a hot burning tip. It will seal the wood pores as it darkens it. The final finish will sit on top of the seared areas and make them glisten. Sear the hooves and dew claws on the deer and the claws on the otters and bears, also.

A Painting Primer

A good paint job can make a good carving great. A bad one can make a good carving worse. Use your painting to enhance your carving, to give it light and shadow, and to give it depth.

Study the colors of your chosen animal and be aware of what time of year it is in your carving. Most animals are lighter in winter so that they blend in with the snowy landscape. Summer coats are richer in color to blend in with the summer foliage.

There are many styles of painting. Wildlife artists use a wide variety of methods, including watercolor, oils, acrylics, colored pencils, markers, and stains. I regularly use acrylic paints and will focus on this method here. The techniques I will discuss are also commonly used with acrylic paints. Of course, you will want to experiment with other painting methods and techniques to achieve different looks. There are so many different styles to choose from; a good class can help. Remember, there is no wrong way or right way to paint... it's up to you to choose.

Painting with Acrylics

Because acrylics dry fast, I find that mixing the colors for each part of the body just before I want to paint that area works best. I usually paint in this order: Head first, neck second, shoulders third, front legs fourth, body fifth, back legs sixth, and tail last.

Mixing acrylics is easy. First put the color on your palette, then fill your brush with water, and touch the brush to the paint. Mix the paint and the water to a milky consistency and apply it like a stain.

Whatever type of paint you choose to use, be sure to keep it thinned. Paint that is too thick will clog up your texturing; paint that is too thin won't provide adequate coverage. Thinning the paint will also let the colors blend together more naturally. These colors can be applied directly to the carving.

Start with the light colors first if you are using acrylic paints. (You'll also want to start with these light colors if you are using water colors. Start with the dark colors first if you are using oil paints.) Then gradually work in the darker colors (or vice versa if you are using oil paints).

Know where your light source is coming from. What areas of your carving will be in shadow and what areas will be hit by the light? You'll want to darken the shadowed areas with a small amount of black added to the base color. Lighter areas can be brightened by adding a small amount of white.

When the animal is all colored the way you want, use up the left over colors on the base so the colors on the animal and its habitat blend together. Mammals are generally colored to blend into their habitat By using your left over colors in this fashion, you can be sure that the colors in your animal match the colors in the habitat perfectly. Plus you have no wasted paint.

Apply the colors quickly, allowing one color to bleed into the next. This technique is commonly called wet-on-wet. Be sure to let all the wet-on-wet dry before you apply the second stage.

Use a stiff-bristled brush to drybrush. Drybrushing will show off the texture you created through carving and woodburning. To drybrush, scrub a color into the brush and pull it gently in the opposite the direction of the hair. Drybrush the base, too.

For the last stage of painting, use a spotter brush to add details like eyes, hooves, claws, nose pads, etc.

Put finish oil, spray Deft or whatever you prefer over the piece after it is totally dry. The finish will sit on top of the seared areas to make them shiny.

The following techniques are commonly used with acrylic paints.
Wet-on-wet: Use this technique to blend two colors. Apply the first color to your carving, then subtly blend in the second color while the first is still wet.
Dry-brushing: Use this technique to give just a hint of color to your painted piece. Use a stiff-bristled brush and apply a small amount of paint lightly to a dried area. Works well for areas with lighter colors. Use also to set off areas the sun would be hitting
Scumbling: A scrubbing motion used to apply paint to the wood. Be careful when scumbling not to ruin subtle texturing.
Glazing: Mix polymer medium with acrylic paints and apply to the carving. Good for creating light colors with a shiny surface and smooth texture.
Lifting: Apply the paint and use a wadded up tissue or a sponge to remove some of the paint. Works great for adding texture to habitat.

Watercolors and salt: Sprinkle salt on wet watercolors. Brush away the crystallized salt for a glistening look. Works well to show snow.
Eyes: Use a detail round brush to paint the colors of the eyes and other details of the face and body. Remember to lighten the upper part of the eyeball where the highlight is.

A Brief Color Study

No matter how accomplished you are at painting, a little knowledge of color theory can go a long way. Color theory is extremely important and will help you to match colors and give your carving depth. The information here is meant to serve only as an introduction. If color theory intrigues you, visit your local library or take an art class to learn more.

Red, blue, and yellow are called primary colors. They are placed in a triangular formation on the color wheel. All colors in the visible spectrum can be made by mixing any combination of these three colors in different proportions.

Mixing any two primary colors in equal proportion will give you a secondary color. For example, mixing yellow and red will give you orange. Combine yellow and blue and you get green. Blue and red yield purple. On the color wheel (see color section), you'll find these secondary colors between the two primaries that are used to create them.

Changing the proportions to favor one or the other of the primary colors will give you a different variation of the secondary color. For example, mix a little red with twice as much blue and you'll get blue-violet. Switch the proportions—add twice as much red and only a little blue—and you'll have red-violet.

Each color has a complementary color located directly opposite it on the wheel. For example, yellow's complement is violet, and red's complement is green. Mixing two complementary colors will yield brown. For different browns, mix different complementary colors.

Using complements in close proximity can make a color seem to glow, or it can make a color dull. To make a color glow, mix its complementary color into the neutral color that surrounds the first color. For example, if you want the yellow eye of an animal to really glow, add a touch of purple (yellow's complementary color) to the black around the yellow eye.

Sunlight on a carving can be shown by mixing a small amount of white with the base color. Show shadows by mixing a small amount of black with the base color. For example, mix the brown of an otter's fur with a small amount of white to show the lighter areas of fur on which the sun is shining. To mix a color for the otter's shadowed areas, add a small amount of black to the brown.

You can also make a color colder or warmer through the careful application of other colors. For example, if you want the cold white snow to appear even colder, add a little purple or blue, cool colors, into the shadows. To make a forest scene warmer, add warm colors, like yellow or orange.

The possibilities are endless when you have a good grasp of color theory.

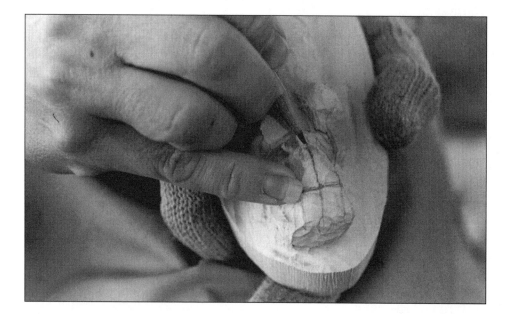

Desiree starts by using a pencil to mark a centerline on the head of her roughed-out otter carving. The centerline begins at the base of the skull and travels the length of the head in a vertical direction. The line acts as a line of symmetry—the otter's facial features are similar on both sides.

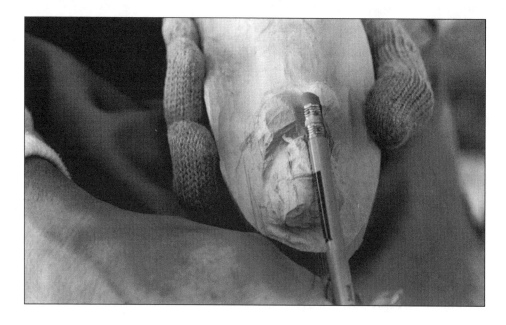

Next, Desiree places the otter's facial features with the help of a pencil. Measuring against her pattern, she uses the pencil to judge space both parallel and perpendicular to the centerline. See accompanying Charts A, B.

River Otter

 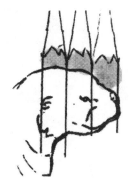 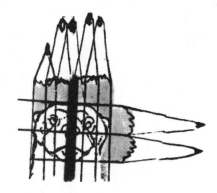

3 pencil widths
top view
side view
front view

2 pencil widths
chin to top of head

Ocean Otter

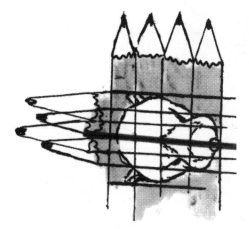  

Ocean otter head is 3 pencil widths across, 2 pencil widths tall and 3 widths long. River otter head is 3 pencil widths across, 2 widths tall and 3 widths long.

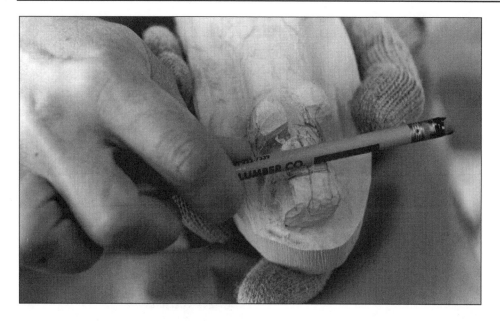

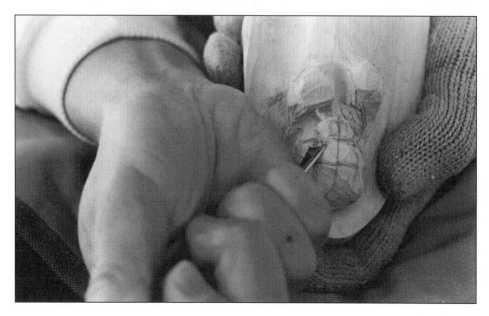

Once she has measured and carefully marked the features of the otter's face, Desiree begins carving. Using a ⅜" #5 gouge, she cuts the wood away from the otter's eye socket. See accompanying Chart C.

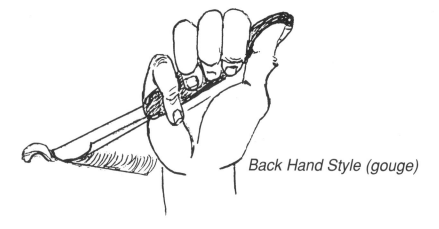

Back Hand Style (gouge)

CHART C

Otter Eyes

River Otter

Side   Front

Ocean Otter

Front   Side

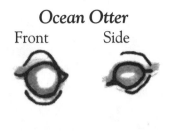
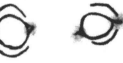

1. Draw and V-cut (use an inverted cone)

2. Inverted pyramid (Tapered cone for power carvers)

3. Undercut (Cylinder for power carvers)

4. Woodburn

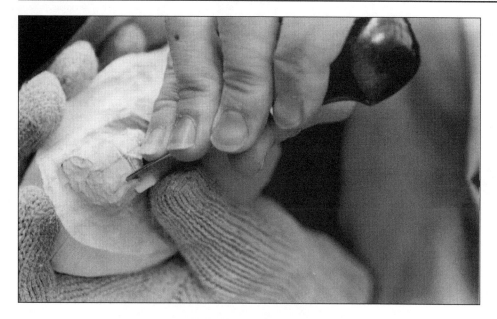

Desiree now carves the temple area in front of the ear and behind the eye socket with the same gouge. She continues to rough carve the face according to her pattern and photographs.

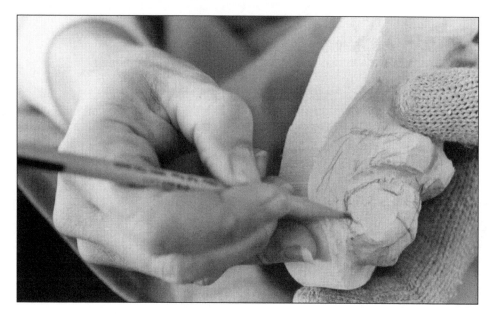

After the face has been roughed out to her satisfaction, Desiree uses her pencil to mark in the facial features once again. Here, she outlines the otter's jaw.

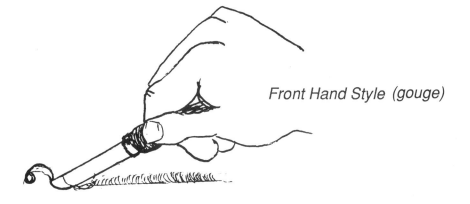

Front Hand Style (gouge)

Next, Desiree pencils in the eyes.

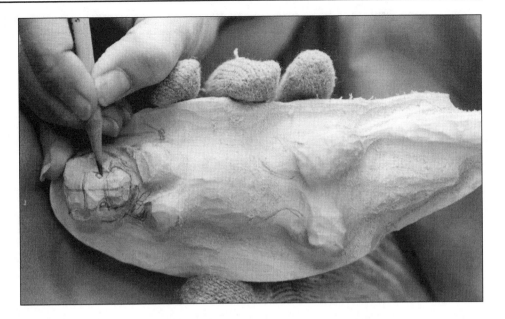

Here, Desiree outlines the otter's nose pad.

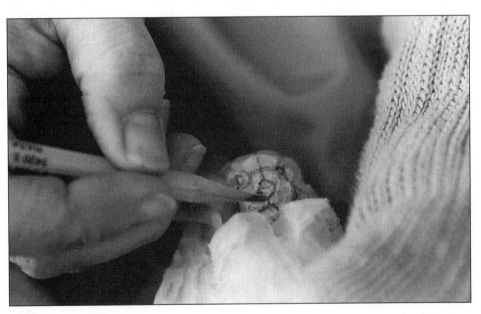

Otter Nose and Chin

River Otter
Front   Side

Ocean Otter
Front   Side

1. Draw and V-cut (inverted cone or knife wheel)

2. Gouge (Ball head rotary bit)

3. Undercut (Cylinder or knife edge wheel)

4. Woodburn

With the facial features penciled in, Desiree continues to rough carve the face and neck area of the otter, referring often to her pattern and photographs. In this photograph she is using a U-gouge to carve around the head and neck. This tool gives a softer cut than a V-gouge.

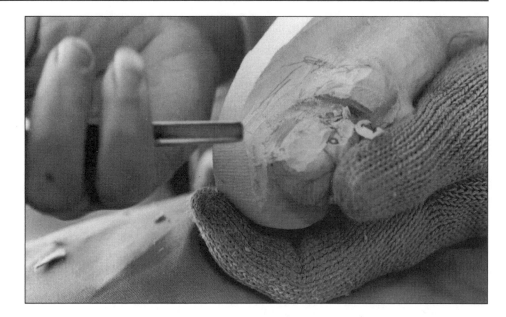

At this point, the face of Desiree's otter is completely rough carved and the facial features are marked in pencil. Desiree is now ready to carve the final details of the face.

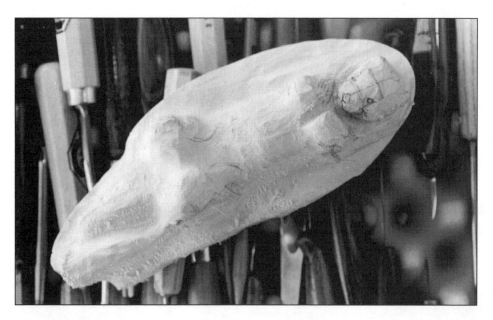

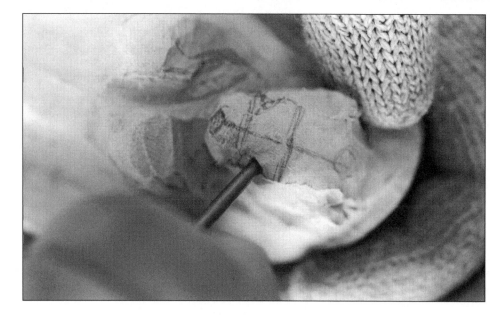

Using a ⅛" diameter eye punch, Desiree creates the otter's right eye. She places the punch directly over the pencil marks for the otter's eye and pushes the tool firmly into the wood. She cautions carvers to remember to punch the eye into the wood following the same angle in which the animal sees. For example, an otter's eye is punched at a 45 degree angle to the centerline.

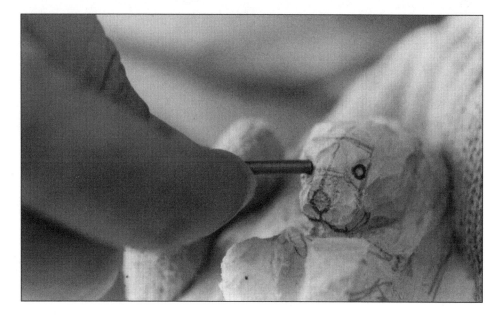

To create the otter's left eye, Desiree repeats the same steps. Again she places the eye punch directly over the penciled-in eye and pushes the tool firmly into the wood at a 45 degree angle.

Still working on the eyes, Desiree uses a detail knife to cut an inverted pyramid inside the eye next to the nose. This cut will indicate the otter's tear duct. She warns carvers not to flick the wood out of the cut because it can cause the wood to tear, resulting in a fuzzy cut. Instead, continue cutting in an inverted pyramid until the knife cuts all the way through.

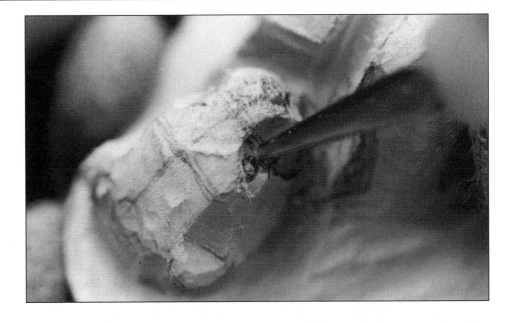

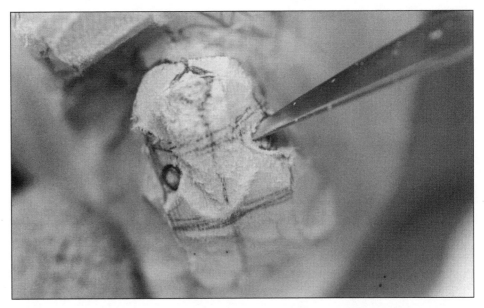

Inverted Pyramid

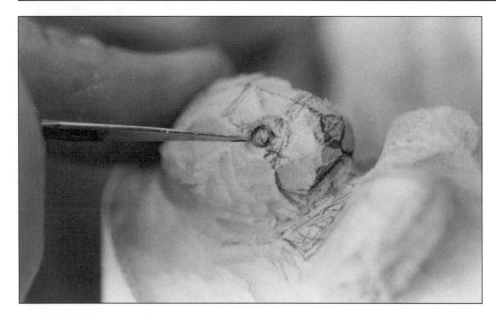

Desiree next uses the detail knife to make a stop cut leading into the otter's temple.

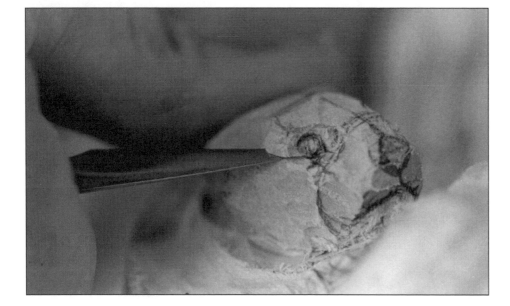

She undercuts the stop cut to remove the sliver of wood at the otter's temple.

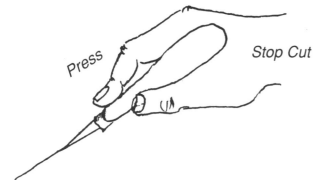

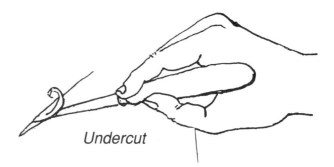

At this point, the otter's face and eye are rough carved. Desiree checks the symmetry of the face so far and moves on to the remaining facial features.

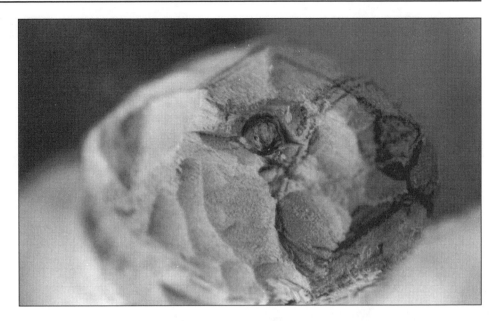

Next, Desiree works on the otter's ears. Again using the detail knife, she carves an inverted pyramid to form the inside of the otter's ear.

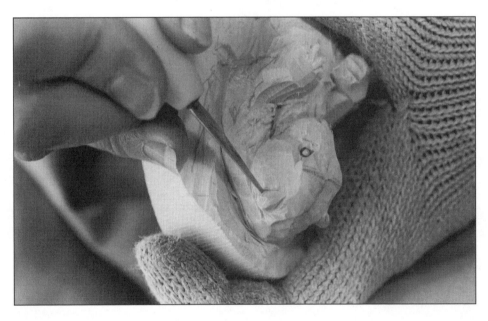

Otter Ears

 1. Draw and trim

 2. Hand carvers use V-tool to shape ear. Power carvers use inverted cone.

 3. Hollow out using a gouge (or a ball bit for power carvers).

 4. Woodburn

To shape the outside of the otter's ear, Desiree uses the detail knife to stop cut and undercut the wood around the ear.

Before detailing the otter's nose, Desiree works to further define the head and neck area. Here, she uses a V-gouge to shape the cleft between the nose and muzzle.

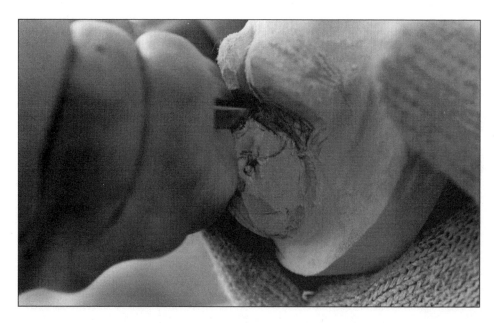

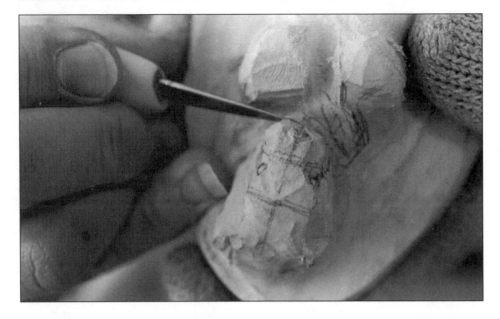

Next, Desiree uses a detail knife to undercut the chin.

She then undercuts the jaw area.

Here, Desiree stop cuts the cheek to hollow out the area underneath.

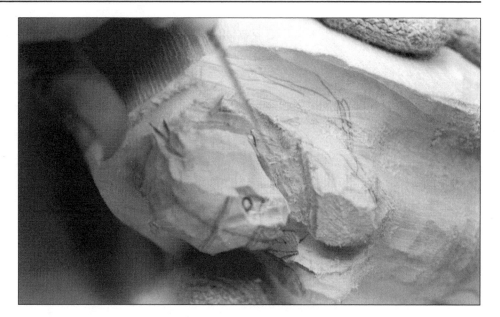

Desiree now begins work on the nose pad. In this photo, she uses a detail knife to undercut the nose pad.

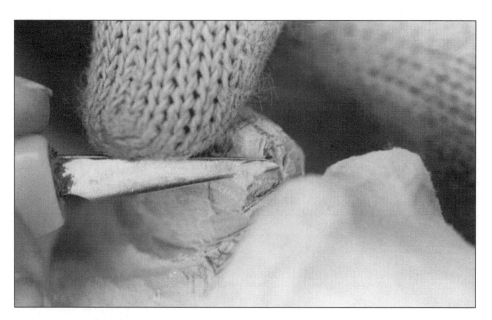

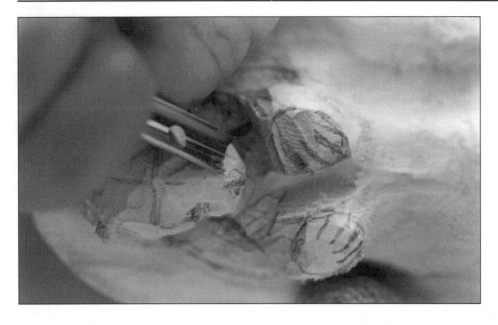

Here, Desiree uses a V-gouge to cut the sides of the nose pad.

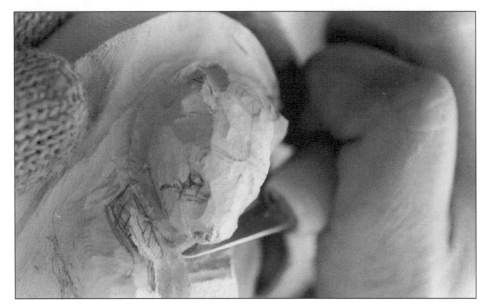

Next, Desiree uses the detail knife to trim up the muzzle. She cautions carvers to pay close attention to their pattern and photographs and not to cut too far in this area. The muzzle must hang over the chin so that the mouth fits underneath.

Here, Desiree uses a detail knife to clean up the fore-head area of the otter's face.

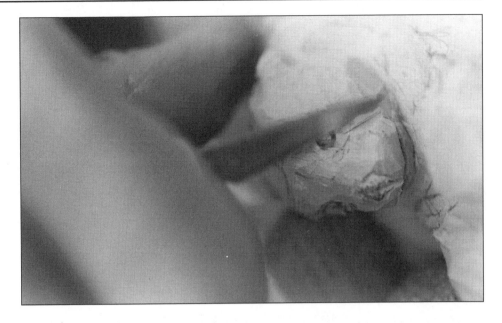

Desiree takes a close look at her progress so far. She carefully checks her work against her pattern and photographs. With the face finished to this point, Desiree moves on to the body.

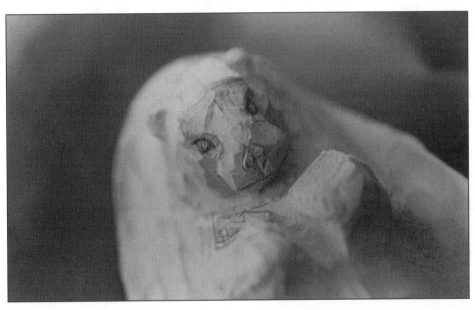

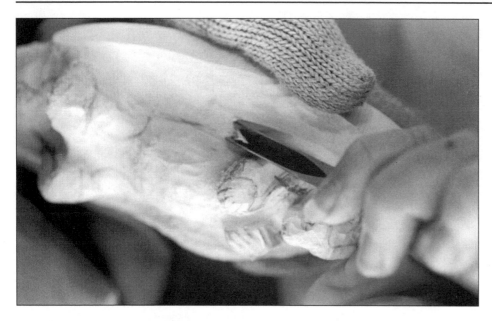

With a V-gouge, Desiree carves out the area between the water and the otter's body to further separate the two.

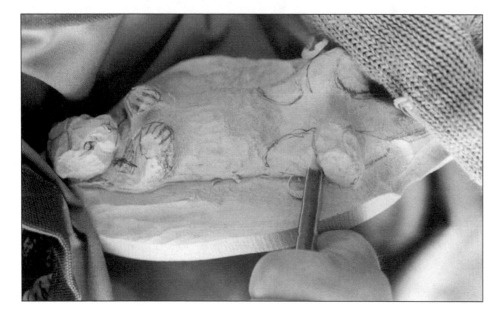

Working on the body, Desiree uses a V-gouge to cut between the otter's shin and his foot.

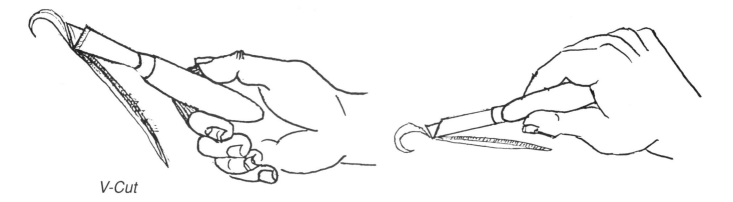

V-Cut

With a U-gouge, Desiree cuts the inside of the upper back leg between the tummy and the knee.

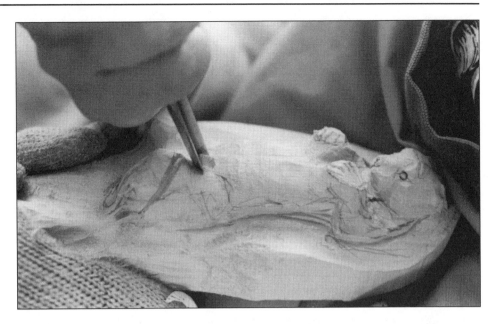

Here, Desiree undercuts the otter's wrist.

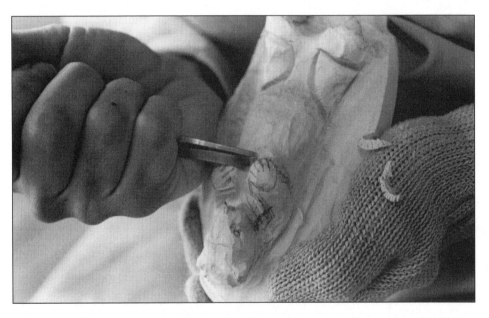

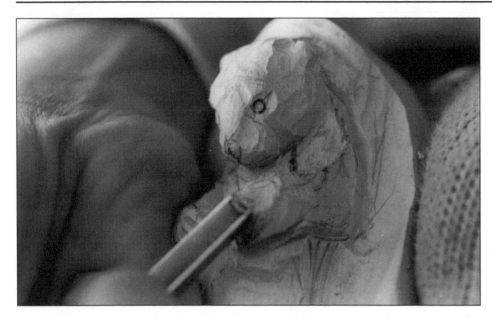

In this photo, Desiree uses a V-gouge to make V-cuts between the otter's toes.

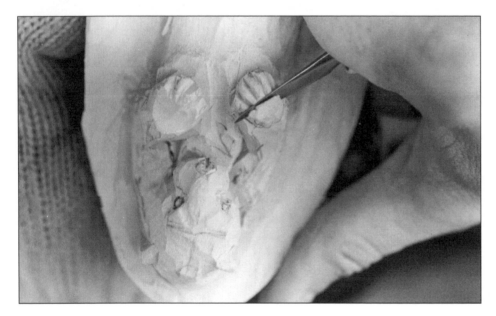

Desiree uses a detail knife to shape the otter's knuckles and wrist.

Otter Feet

River Otter   **Ocean Otter**

1. Draw trim

2. V-cut (inverted cone). Hand carvers use V-cut to define toes. Power carvers use inverted cone.

3. Shape toes adding the detail you want.

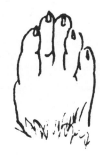

4. Woodburn (sear claws)

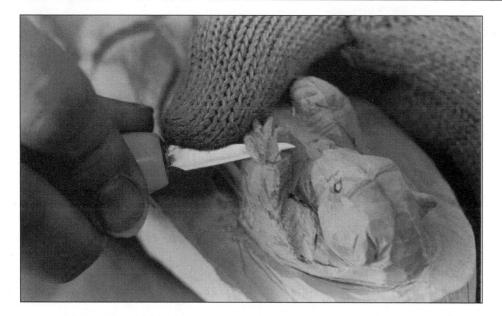

Continuing to work on the otter's paws, Desiree further undercuts the paws with a detail knife. She warns carvers not to press down too much as this is a weak area of the carving. It is all too easy to pop off the paw under too much pressure.

1. Desiree begins painting the otter once she has completed all the woodburning. Starting at the head and continuing on to its tail, Desiree uses a big soft brush to add a brown color all over the otter. The colors she uses are acrylic and mixed to match the colors she sees on photographs of the otter. Desiree cautions carvers not to add too much water when mixing paints. Paint should be of a milky consistency. Too much water may cause the wood to swell and subtle texture can become lost.

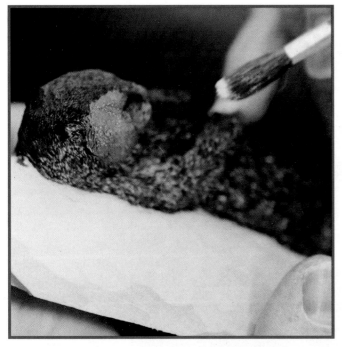

2. Desiree begins to add additional colors using a wet-on-wet technique. Here she added color to the face. Placing the colors side by side when they are both still wet will allow the colors to blend into one another.

3. Desiree uses the wet-on-wet technique to blend colors for the otter's head. Notice the milky consistency of the paint.

Mammals:
An Artistic Approach
by Desiree Hajny

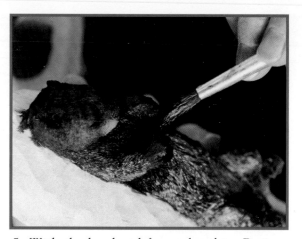

4. Still working on the head, Desiree uses a darker color to show shadows on the face.

5. With the head and face colored in, Desiree moves on to the otter's tummy. Here again she uses a wet-on-wet technique to add color to the otter's body. She cautions carvers not to use too much paint. Too much will obscure the subtle texturing underneath.

6. According to the photographs of the otter that Desiree is using for reference the otter's tail is a lighter color than it's body. She mixes a lighter brown and applies it to the tail. She uses a wet-on-wet technique so that the color of the tail will blend into the color of the body.

8. To color the base, Desiree mixes colors used on the otter. In this manner, she can be sure the animal will blend into it's habitat as it does in nature. The green you see here is actually a blend of black and yellow used in the browns on the otter.

7. Desiree adds highlights to the areas of her carving where the sun hits the otter by mixing a bit of white with the base color and blending it in.

Mammals:
An Artistic Approach
by Desiree Hajny

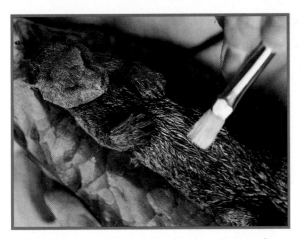

9. To create highlights and make the colors uniform, Desiree drybrushes the carving. Here, she loads a stiff brush with a small amount of color and scrubs it into the texture.She works in the opposite direction of the flow of the fur. Desiree cautions carvers not to scrub too hard; this practice may cause damage to subtle texturing.

10. Desiree also drybrushes the base. Drybrushing the base will soften colors and give the base and the otter a uniform cast.

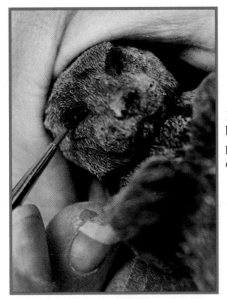

11. Using a spotter brush, Desiree paints in the otter's eye.

12. She uses the same technique to add detail to the otter's nose.

13. Using a small amount of white, Desiree uses the spotter brush to add a highlight to the otter's eye. She uses this same method to create highlights on the otter's nose as well.

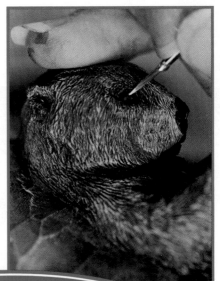

Mammals:
An Artistic Approach
by Desiree Hajny

14. Desiree places three different otter carvings side by side to show how different colors can be used to paint the otter.

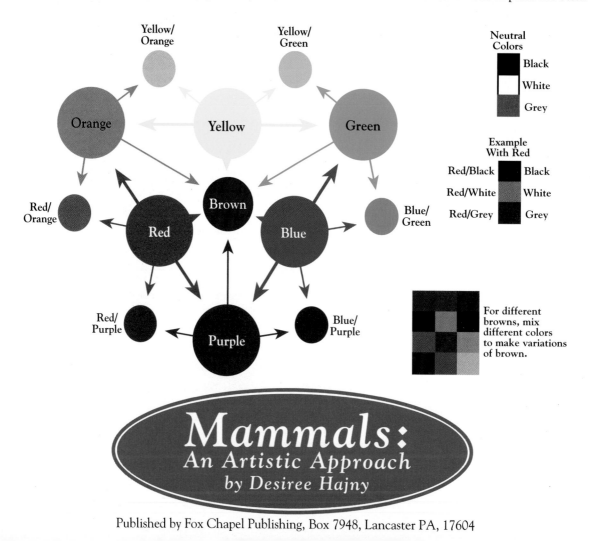

Yellow/Orange

Yellow/Green

Orange

Yellow

Green

Neutral Colors

Black

White

Grey

Brown

Red/Orange

Red

Blue

Blue/Green

Example With Red

Red/Black — Black

Red/White — White

Red/Grey — Grey

Red/Purple

Purple

Blue/Purple

For different browns, mix different colors to make variations of brown.

Mammals:
An Artistic Approach
by Desiree Hajny

Published by Fox Chapel Publishing, Box 7948, Lancaster PA, 17604

Next, Desiree undercuts the wrist area of the otter's paw. Again, she cautions carvers to be very careful in carving this delicate area.

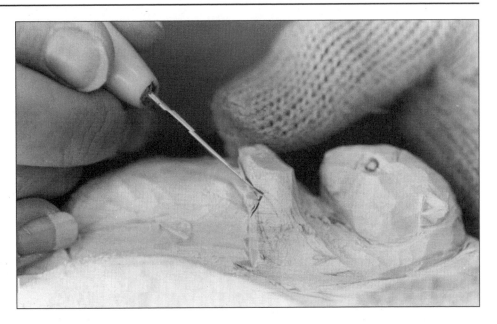

Desiree now moves to the otter's lower heels and uses a detail knife to shape them.

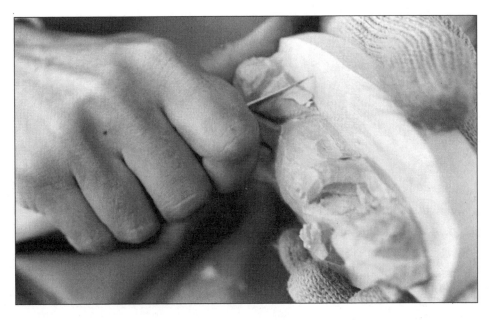

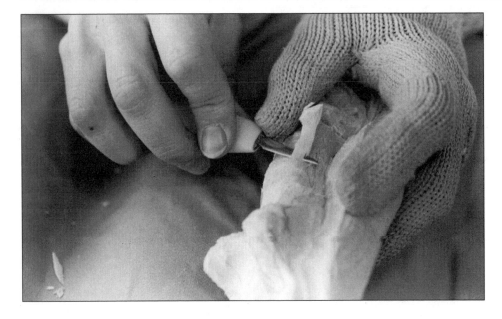

She shapes the lower paws in the same fashion as the upper paws.

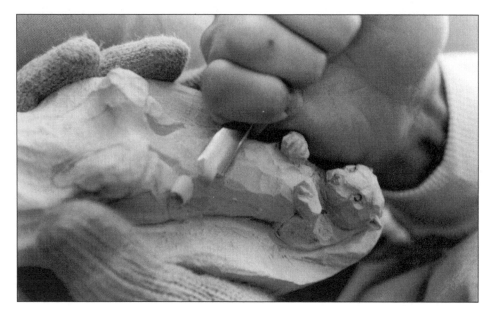

With the paws shaped, Desiree moves on to the otter's belly. Here, she uses a #6 gouge to begin shaping the belly.

Once the belly is shaped to Desiree's satisfaction, she uses a V-gouge and V-cuts to add texture to the belly. She crosses her cuts as much as possible to help give the illusion of fur.

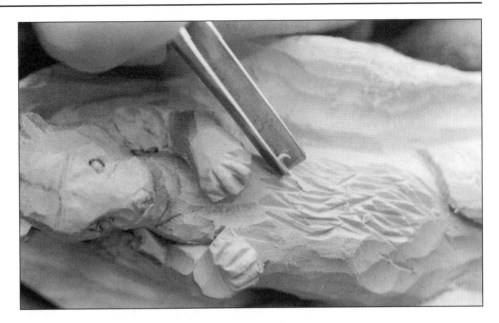

After Desiree finishes texturing with the gouge, she moves on to woodburning. Using tip 10A, Desiree burns the otter's eyes. See Chart C for an outline.

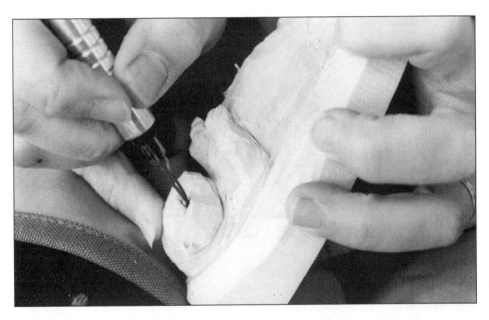

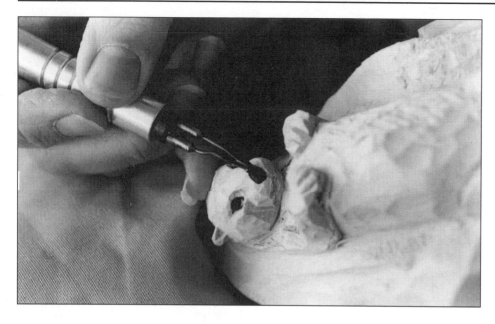

Still using tip 10A, Desiree next burns the otter's nose.

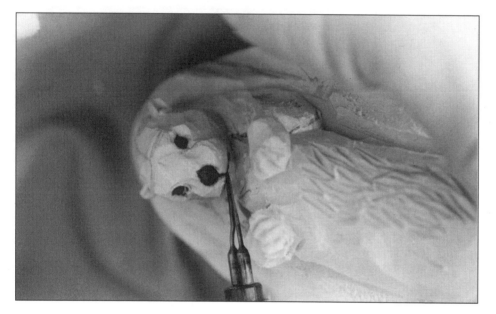

Desiree burns the otter's mouth and the cleft between the nose and mouth with the same tip.

Tip 10A is also used to burn in the whiskers on the otter's face.

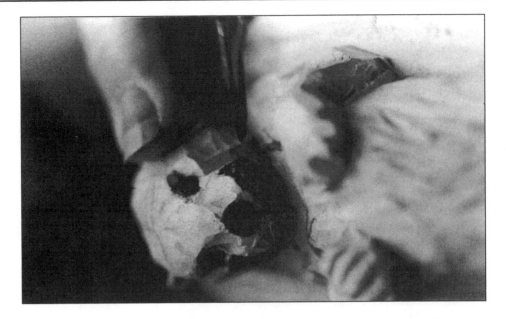

Here, she burns in the otter's eyelid.

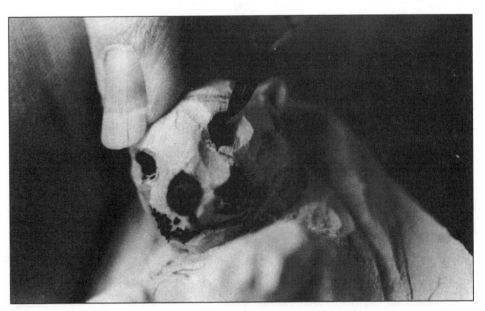

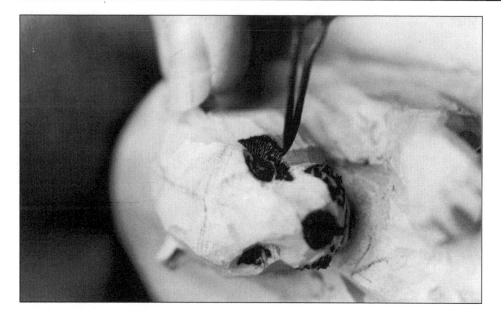

Desiree continues to woodburn the otter's face. She uses short strokes to burn in fur. She starts at the eye and burns outward in the direction of the fur's flow.

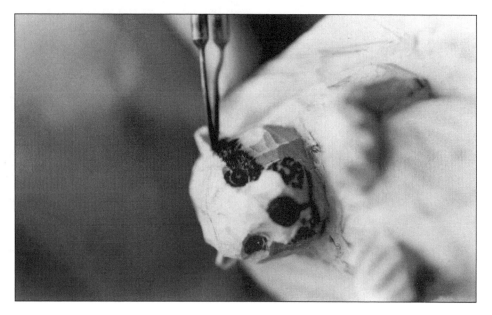

Desiree moves along the temple, burning in fur with short strokes.

The river otter has a sleek body with a thick tapering tail, a long round head with prominent whiskers, small ears and short legs with four fully webbed feet.

Ocean otters are built pretty much the same as the river otter except they have a flat tail that tapers. The river otter has clawed feet and the ocean otter has stubby toes. Their nose shapes are different and their coloration is different.

River Otter

Ocean Otter

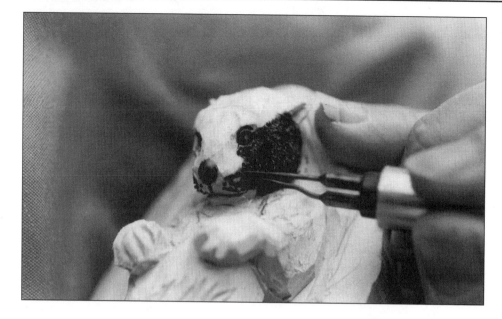

Desiree fills in the side of the face with woodburned texture. Here strokes are short, but cross over each other frequently to give the illusion of fur.

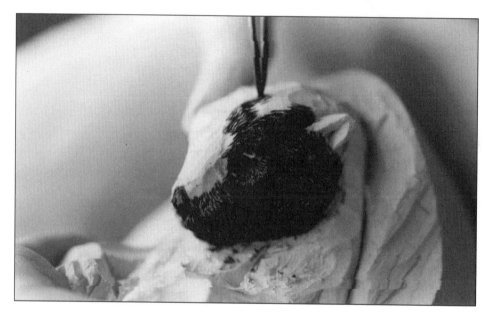

At this point, Desiree is still woodburning the fur on the otter's face. The direction of the otter's fur changes subtly here at the otter's temple.

Desiree fills in the area between the temple and the top of the head with the same short, cross-over strokes.

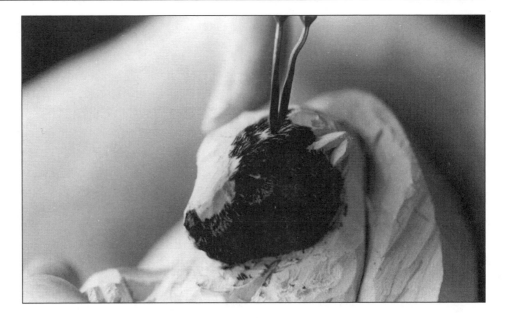

Here, Desiree burns the inside of the otter's ear with tip 10A.

Desiree moves on to woodburn the otter's tummy. She is again using tip 10A and works in longer, cross-over strokes.

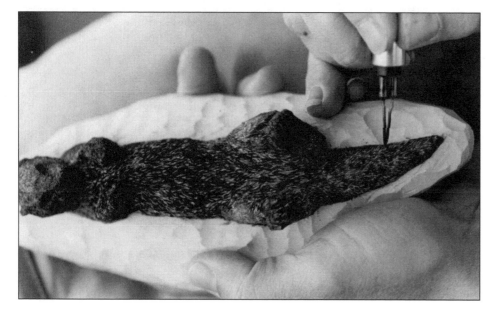

Desiree finishes by woodburning the otter's tail with the same basic strokes.

A close-up look at the finished burn marks on the otter's face.

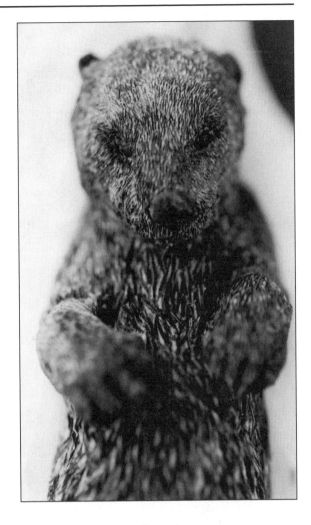

Different Texturing Approaches

V-Cut   **U Gouge (Veiner)**   **Rotary Bit**

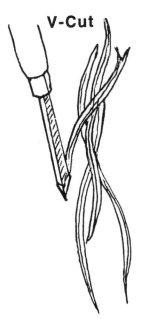

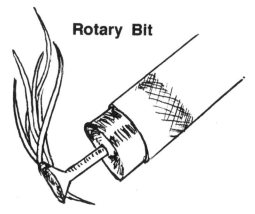

Rotary Tips: Inverted Cone, Knife-Edge Wheel
Palm Tools: V-Cut, Veiners (Deep U Gouge),
V-Parting Tool

Always remember gravity pulls hair downward. The hair is curved, not straight. It also crosses over other hairs. Twist your wrist for curves.

Woodburning

Press and pull in the direction of the hair. Cross over softly. Use a stab-pull motion for short hairs.

For the eye, use the point along the outside of the eyeball, then, with the flat side, sear the sphere of the eyeball.

Use the same technique for hooves, dew claws and claws.

Common Burning Mistakes

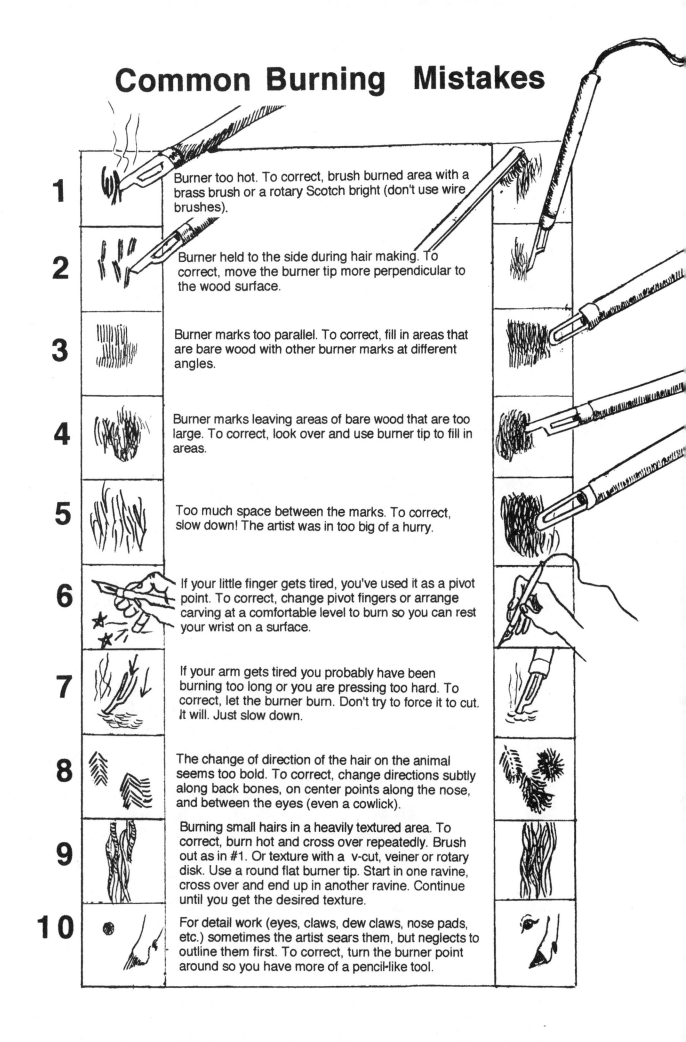

1 Burner too hot. To correct, brush burned area with a brass brush or a rotary Scotch bright (don't use wire brushes).

2 Burner held to the side during hair making. To correct, move the burner tip more perpendicular to the wood surface.

3 Burner marks too parallel. To correct, fill in areas that are bare wood with other burner marks at different angles.

4 Burner marks leaving areas of bare wood that are too large. To correct, look over and use burner tip to fill in areas.

5 Too much space between the marks. To correct, slow down! The artist was in too big of a hurry.

6 If your little finger gets tired, you've used it as a pivot point. To correct, change pivot fingers or arrange carving at a comfortable level to burn so you can rest your wrist on a surface.

7 If your arm gets tired you probably have been burning too long or you are pressing too hard. To correct, let the burner burn. Don't try to force it to cut. It will. Just slow down.

8 The change of direction of the hair on the animal seems too bold. To correct, change directions subtly along back bones, on center points along the nose, and between the eyes (even a cowlick).

9 Burning small hairs in a heavily textured area. To correct, burn hot and cross over repeatedly. Brush out as in #1. Or texture with a v-cut, veiner or rotary disk. Use a round flat burner tip. Start in one ravine, cross over and end up in another ravine. Continue until you get the desired texture.

10 For detail work (eyes, claws, dew claws, nose pads, etc.) sometimes the artist sears them, but neglects to outline them first. To correct, turn the burner point around so you have more of a pencil-like tool.

THE DEER

The deer is an all-time favorite subject of wildlife artists throughout the ages, and I'm no exception. Its graceful lines and genteel manner make for an interesting subject, not just for the viewer, but for the carver as well. Unfortunately, the graceful lines and thin legs and hooves of the deer also make it an intimidating subject for beginning carvers. Here again, knowing your subject thoroughly can help to calm your fears.

I will describe the white-tailed deer and the mule deer briefly here. Before you start carving, you'll want to do some additional research on your own. Start with books and videos at your local library. Museums and zoos are also good places to find reference material. Remember, though, that taxidermists who make museum models can sometimes make mistakes if they are not familiar with the animal. Also remember that zoo animals never exactly resemble their wild counterparts. Most are better fed and better groomed than deer in the wild.

The white-tailed deer is the most abundant hoofed mammal in North America. It lives in mixed woodlands, in second growth forests, and at the forest's edge. Adult white tails are tawny above in summer with white below. In winter, their coats change to blue-gray above with white below. The white tail is the only eastern deer with a tail that is white below and the same color as the back above. The antlers of the white tail have erect unbranched tines arising from a main base.

In addition to being a graceful animal, the white-tailed deer is also very nervous and skittish. When startled into flight, it will raise its tail like a sort of flag to show the white below. To escape an enemy, it will often run downhill to get away faster.

The mule deer lives in open forests, brush areas, and rocky uplands. Its coat appears reddish-brown in summer and brownish-gray in winter. During both seasons, its belly, throat patch, and rump patch are white in color. The mule deer's ears are much larger than those of the white tail. In addition, its tail is rope-like with a black tip.

Mule deer have a jumping gait and carry their tails down at all times. They are calm and curious by nature and will often avoid areas of human activity. When pursued, they take the opposite path of the white tail and run up an incline to tire out their enemy.

Mammals: An Artistic Approach

Mammals: An Artistic Approach

Planning to Carve a Deer

After you have chosen which species of deer to carve and have researched the animal thoroughly, it is time to plan your carving. Once again, I must stress that it is important to understand the ani-

mal thoroughly before you attempt to carve it. Understanding the animal will help you to adapt your sculpture to the wood's grain. You'll be able to match the bends of the deer with the bends of the wood and better capture the essence of the animal.

Remember, too, that each deer has its own personality and its own features. Like us, some have longer noses, wider noses, wider set eyes, or larger ears. Also remember that everything about your deer will play a part in your carving. Is it winter or summer? Coats change color from season to season. Is it spring or fall? Antlers will be velvety in the spring and bony in the fall, and the buck's neck will be thicker, more muscled, in order to support the weight of the antlers. Was it a bad winter? If so, your animal will be thin.

You will find that the patterns in this chapter are designed to make you work on studying your subject. The patterns provided are does with fawns. Each pattern has a side view of the buck's head to

help you redesign. The white tail pattern shows the animal slightly smaller than the mule deer pattern. Don't be afraid of using a photocopy machine to help you enlarge or shrink a pattern.

You can also redraw any of these patterns into a walking deer by using the walking chart and the skeleton sketch in this chapter. The highlighted joints show how a deer's joints move when it walks. Notice how the shoulder moves up when it is supporting the weight. The same thing happens with the hips. The leg also shifts under the body when it is supporting the weight. Chart U shows how the backbone, which is fused to the pelvis, moves along with the pelvis whenever the animal moves. The next chart, Chart V, shows how the pelvis shifts right along with the step. The deer's shoulders are not fused to the backbone, but they are connected to it by tendons and ligaments and will move with a turn or weight shift. See how important anatomy is to planning your carving!

Carving Notes

If you are carving the standing doe and fawn, transfer your pattern to a 7" x 5½" x 3¼" block of wood with the grain running vertically.

If your are carving the lying-down doe and fawn, trace the pattern onto a 4" x 6¾" x 3½" block of wood with the grain running vertically.

If you have altered the pattern, make sure you allowed enough wood for shifts in the joints and balance, the curve of the spine, and other alterations.

Eye sockets are 45 degrees from the centerline.

Use Charts W through Y to draw the face.

Use Charts Z to change the position of the ears.

Vary the facial expression by moving the chin to the side for grazing.

Notice on Chart S there is a hollow area above the femur. Gouge this area out slightly with a #10 gouge or a Tree Radius Small (¾") bit.

Use Charts A2 and A3 to carve the feet.

Split the hoof up the middle with a v-cut or rotary inverted cone. Remember the surface of the hooves and dew claws is coming from inside the foot. The fur and skin hang over the feet.

Antlers have always caused a lot of problems for woodcarvers, so I have taken the liberty to learn several different techniques from several different artists and share some with you. The problem with carving antlers is dealing with the changing grains. To deal with the weak points, I superglue those areas. Other artists use harder woods and insert them later. Some make a wire frame and put bread dough or clay over the wire. Some leave the tines together until all is completed and then carefully use a rotary cutter to cut them, supergluing afterwards. The most interesting way I discovered was laminating veneer crisscross and cutting antlers out of that, then carving them with different rotary bits and inserting them later—no weak points. You are free to choose.

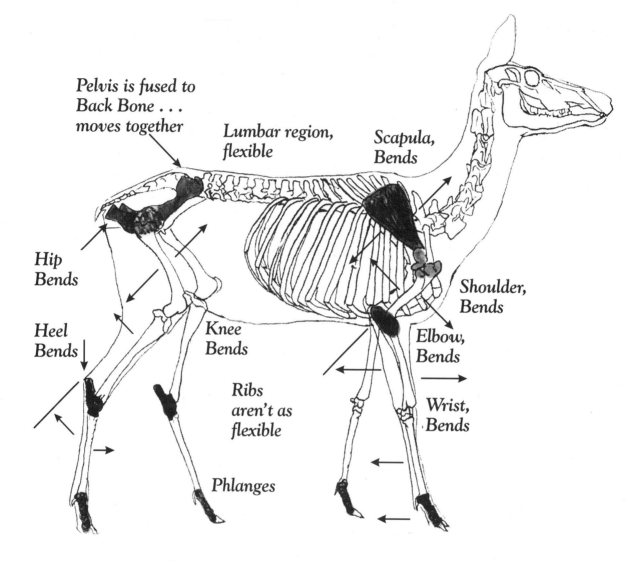

Pelvis is fused to
Back Bone . . .
moves together

Lumbar region,
flexible

Scapula,
Bends

Hip
Bends

Heel
Bends

Knee
Bends

Shoulder,
Bends

Elbow,
Bends

Wrist,
Bends

Ribs
aren't as
flexible

Phlanges

Notice the shift in the deer's joints as it moves.

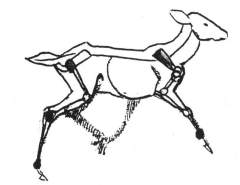

CHART T

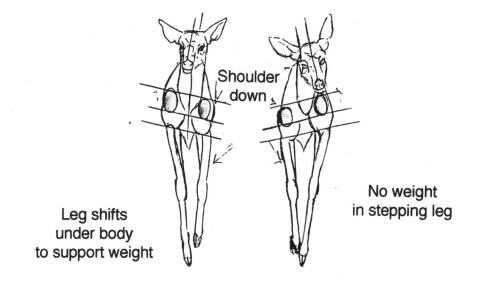

Shoulder down

Leg shifts
under body
to support weight

No weight
in stepping leg

CHART U

Backbone shifts; it is fused
at a right angle to the hips

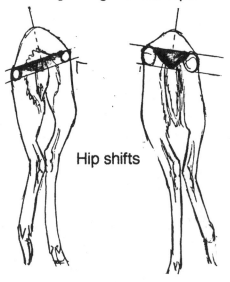

Hip shifts

Leg shifts
under body
to support weight

CHART V

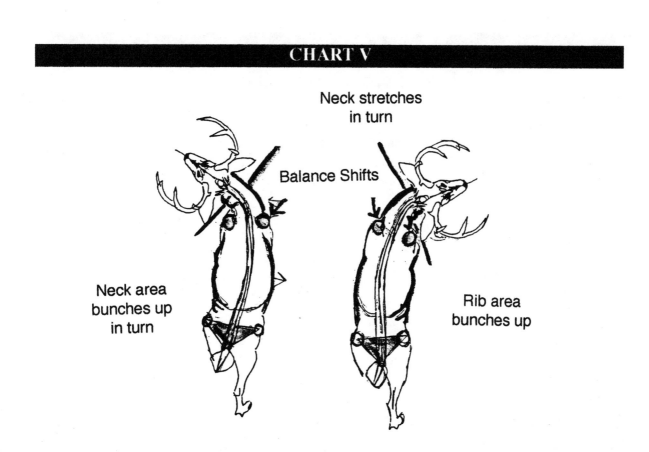

Neck stretches
in turn

Balance Shifts

Neck area
bunches up
in turn

Rib area
bunches up

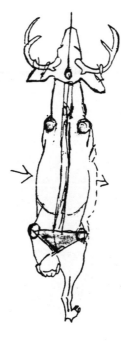

Most hoofed mammals
walk with their hind foot
placed behind the imprint
of their front foot,
or often right in the imprint

Deer Eyes: Carving Tips

Side   *Front*

1. Draw, trim and V-cut (knife edge or wheel or inverted wide cone if using rotary tools)

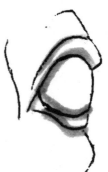

2. Corners of eyes—inverted pyramid cut. Power carvers use tapered cutter.

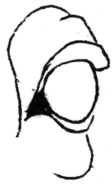

3. Undercut (knife point or a cylinder cutter).

4. Woodburn

CHART X

Deer Nose and Mouth: Carving Tips

1. Draw, trim and V-cut (knife edge wheel or inverted wide cone if using rotary tools)

2. Gouge (ball for rotary tools)

3. Undercut (cylinder or inverted cone)

4. Woodburn

Carving and Burning Deer Ears

1. Draw and trim

2. V-Cut with chisel. Power carvers use knife edge wheel or inverted cone ball.

3. Use gouges to remove wood. Power carvers will use ball.

4. Woodburn

Ear Anatomy

Cartilage connected to the skull located above the pivot point of jaw area where it fits into the skull. ○

This area stays connected to the skull, but turns the ears so the animal can constantly be on alert for danger.

The shaping of the ear is pear shaped with a hollowed out center. The pear shape sits on the sphere like cartilage.

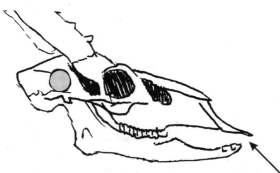

It lacks upper front teeth, tough pad is there instead.

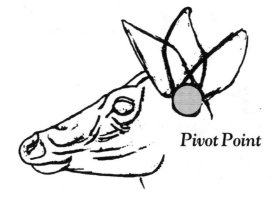

Pivot Point

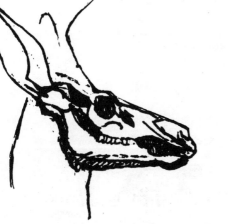

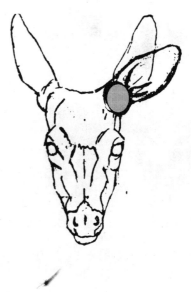

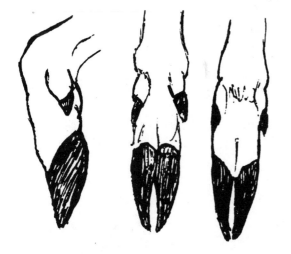

Whitetail deer *Deer running*

Hind *Front*

Notice dew claws are further from hooves on the hind foot.

Dewclaws will show on cloven hooved animals when running.

Toes will be splayed

Back hoof fits into front hoof print.

Drag marks will appear in deep snow when walking.

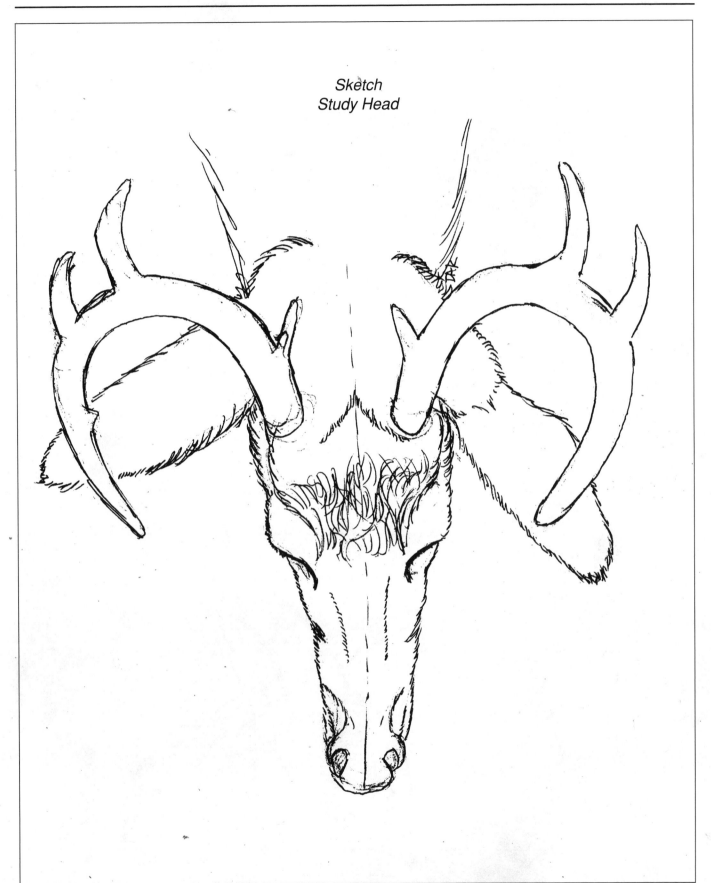

Sketch
Study Head

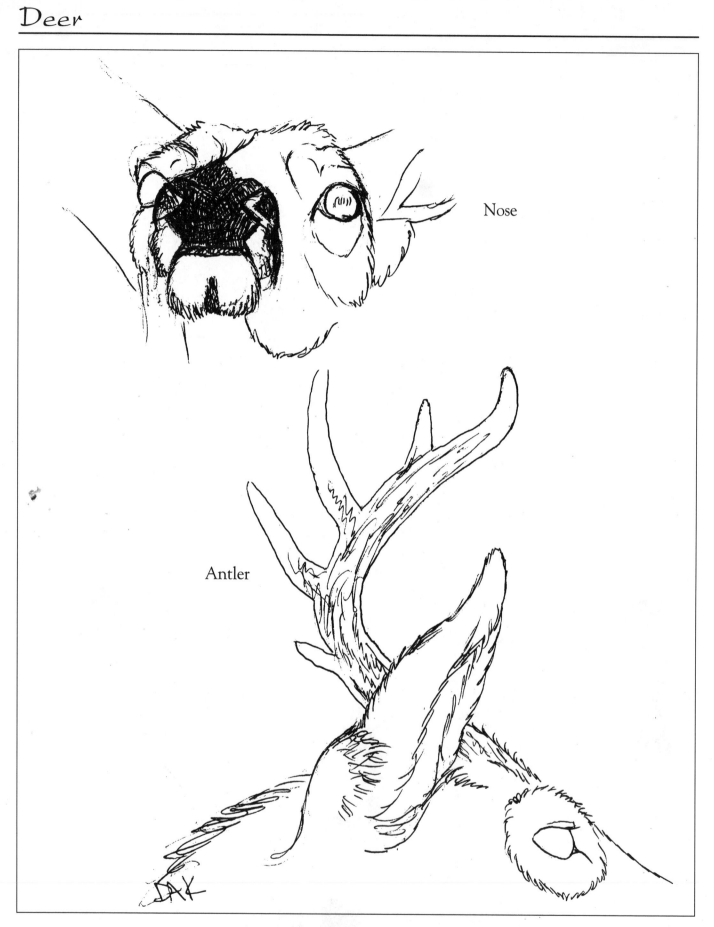

Nose

Antler

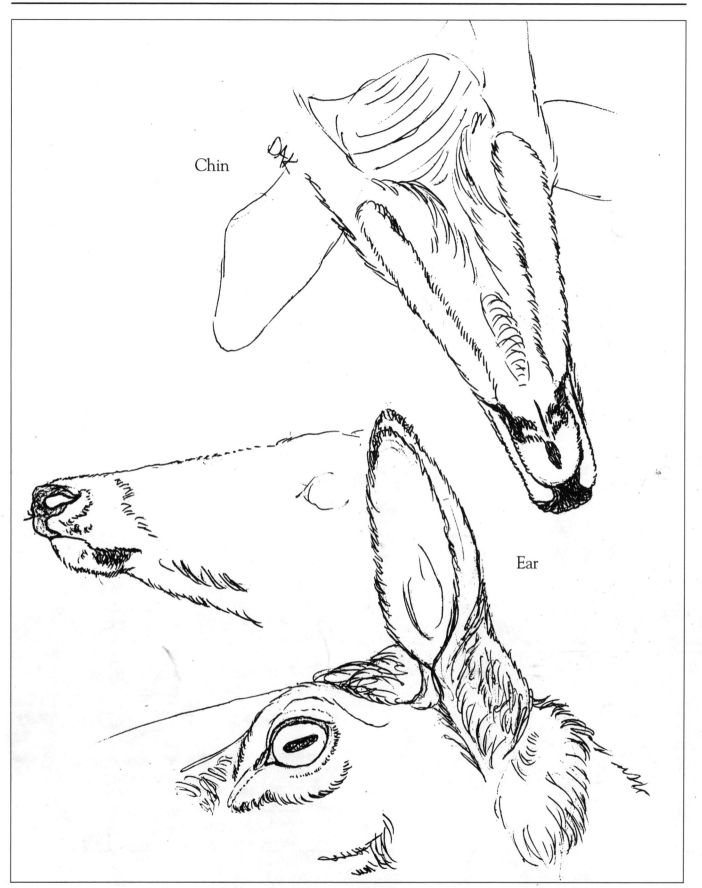

Chin

Ear

Carving Antlers

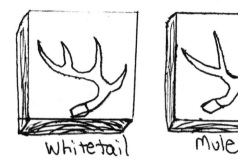

Whitetail   Mule

1. Cut out two side-view antlers with a scroll saw, band saw or jewelers saw. Or cut out one antler in double thickness and saw it in half.

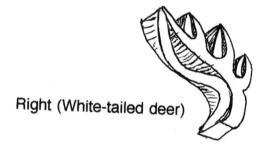

Right (White-tailed deer)

2. Mark in the front view of the antlers (left and right).

3. Remove unwanted wood with a large round burr. Brace the antler against wood or a hard surface (not slick) and take your time.

4. With each tine you work on, try to support it on the hard surface.

5. For final shaping, use abrasives.

6. When completed, attach the antler to the head. Drill sockets and insert the elongated base of the antler. Glue it in with wood glue. Make sure the right and left antlers are inserted appropriately. For a better look, trim the base with a shoulder (optional).

Antlers

MULE DEER BUCK IN FALL

MULE DEER BUCK IN VELVET

WHITE TAIL BUCK IN FALL

WHITE TAIL BUCK IN VELVET

White tailed deer hair tract

White tailed fawn

Antlers

MULE DEER BUCK IN FALL

MULE DEER BUCK IN VELVET

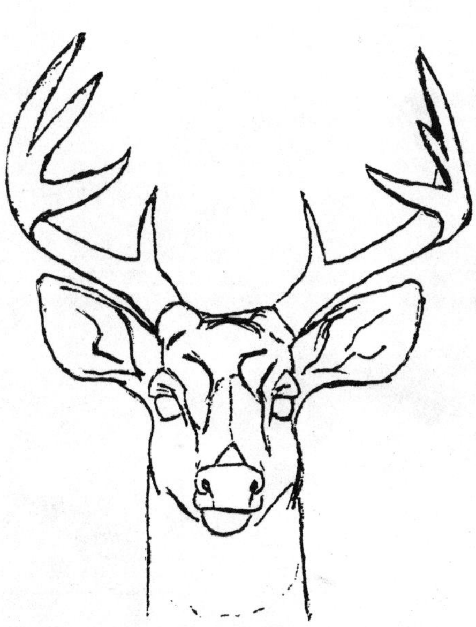

WHITE TAIL BUCK IN FALL

WHITE TAIL BUCK IN VELVET

White tailed deer hair tract

White tailed fawn

Mule deer hair tract

Mule deer fawn

White Tail Deer and Mule Deer

Antlers of a mule deer are small forks on larger forks. Antlers of a white tail sweep upward, outward and forward. The tines grow off the main beam.

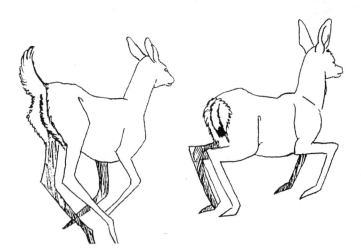

Deer are lightly muscled and built for speed. White tails lope gracefully in flight. Mule deer walk stiff legged and puff themselves up to make themselves larger. The mule deer is a heavier build than the white tail.

Tails are different. A white tail's tail is dark when down and white underneath. The white only shows when the deer is in distress. The mule deer tail is white with a black tip. The rump area is also white.

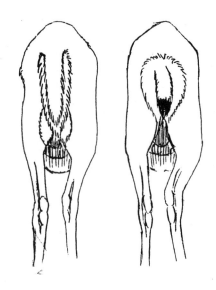

Relaxing Mule Doe and Fawn

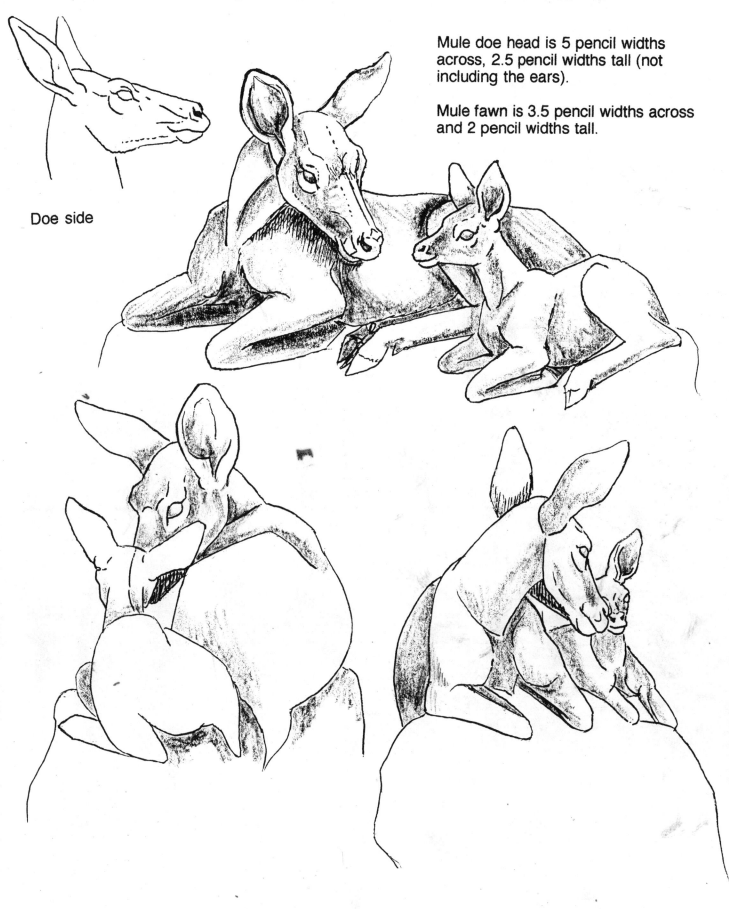

Mule doe head is 5 pencil widths across, 2.5 pencil widths tall (not including the ears).

Mule fawn is 3.5 pencil widths across and 2 pencil widths tall.

Doe side

Standing White Tail Doe and Fawn

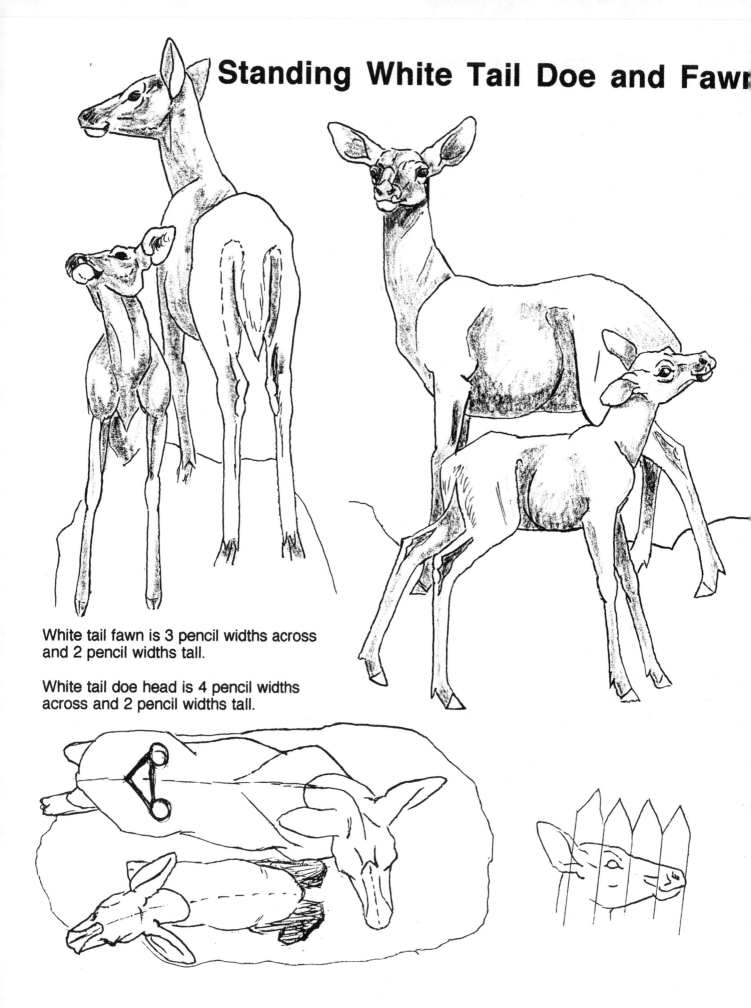

White tail fawn is 3 pencil widths across and 2 pencil widths tall.

White tail doe head is 4 pencil widths across and 2 pencil widths tall.

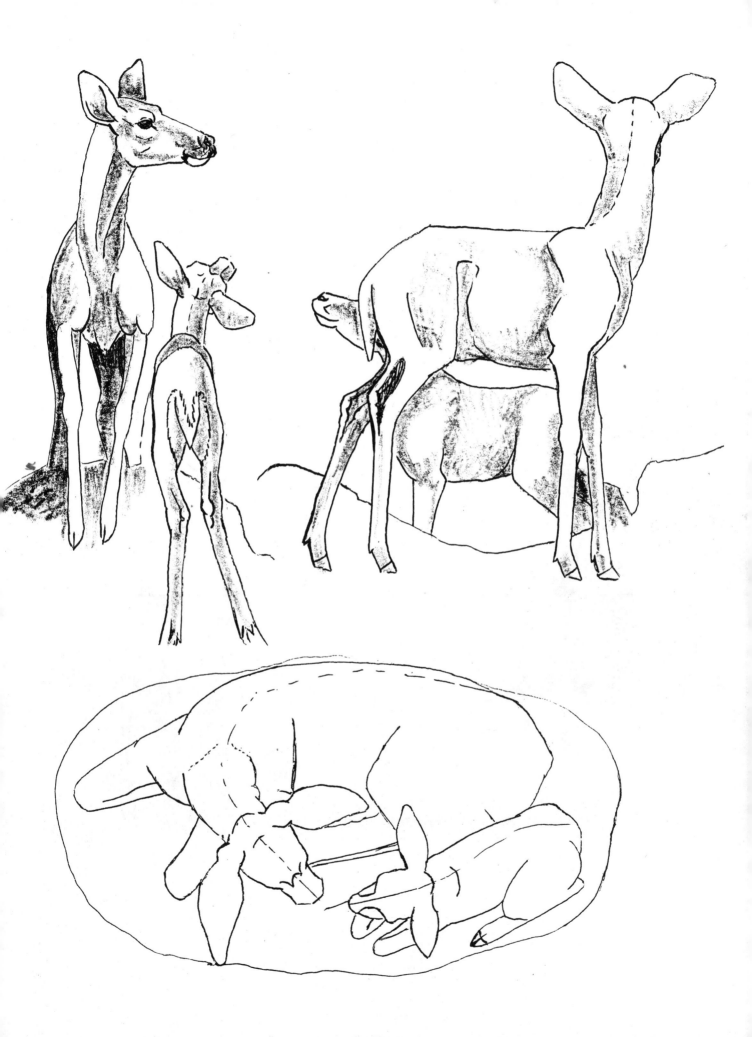

Moose

Body and head, dark brown. Legs,
cream white. Antlers vary from golden
brown to dark brown.

Elk

Head, under belly, neck, shoulders and
legs are dark blackish brown. Body is
tan with white rump. Chin and around
nose pad, white.

Insert → SIDE

SIDE

Pronghorn

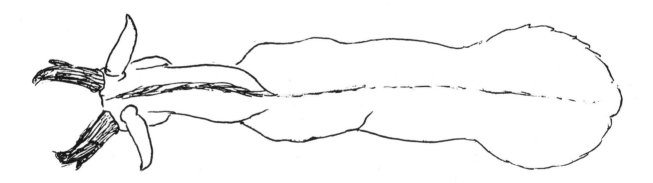

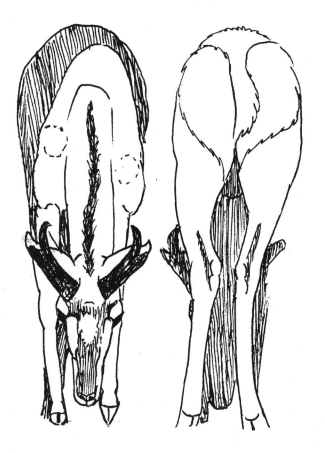

White patches on the neck, throat, inside of ears, belly, rump, inside of legs and sometimes outside of legs, too. Brown tail.

Goldish tan (sometimes reddish tan). Black eyes. Around ears males have black. Horns black.

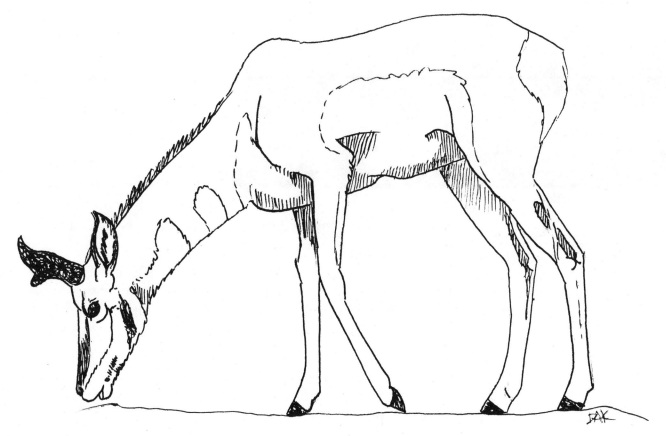

THE BEAR
Black, Grizzly, and Polar

The bear is a very intimidating carving subject for beginning carvers because of its bulk. It is a huge animal—the largest living carnivore. Its artistic lines are very bold and daunting, not yielding and inviting like the otter.

But choosing a bear as your subject can be very rewarding. Its anatomy is very familiar, more human-like, which can make understanding the way the bear moves much easier. For example, a bear walks on his entire foot, from heel to toe, similar to the way you and I walk. And a bear openly expresses many facets of its personality. A mother bear whose cubs are in danger can appear very ferocious. But that same mother bear can later exhibit a tender playfulness with her cubs.

I will describe the black bear, the polar bear, and the grizzly bear briefly here, but you'll want to do more research on your own before you start your carving. Look for information in books and videos at your local library. Museums are a good place to find mounted specimens. You can also find animals to study at zoos, but remember that the care these animals are given will change their appearance when compared to wild animals. Zoo bears will be better fed and better groomed than a wild bear.

The black bear, the smallest and most common bear of the three, is found throughout the forests and wooded areas of Alaska and Canada and in parts of the western and eastern United States. Its fur varies in color from black on the east coast to cinnamon on the west coast. A white patch is commonly found on its throat. The black bear has no shoulder hump and curved, black claws. The black bear's nose is usually dark in color, though sometimes it varies to brownish pink.

The grizzly, of the brown bear family, lives on the tundra and in the forests of Alaska and western Canada. Its fur ranges in color from yellowish to dark brown to black and is flecked with black. It, unlike the black bear, sports a shoulder hump and a scooped-out forehead. Its claws are crayon length and straighter and are dark when the animal is young, but gradually get lighter as the bear ages.

The polar bear lives on the arctic plains. Its fur is white, and in the summer, it sometimes takes on a yellowish tinge. A young polar bear is whiter than an older adult. The polar bear's nose pad and eyes are black, and its claws are curved and black. Its strong shoulders, stream-lined body, thick, oily fur, and webbed paws make it an excellent swimmer.

Planning to Carve a Bear

Now that you've conducted your research and are thoroughly versed in "bear," you are ready to plan your carving. Again, remember that each bear has its own personality and its own unique features.

Some will have longer noses; others will have deeper set eyes. Make your bear unique, but be careful not to exaggerate the features too much. You want your bear to look realistic.

Also remember that everything about your bear will impact your carving. For example, what time of year it is will play an important role in what your bear looks like. Bears that live in areas with harsh winters hibernate. So in the fall, to prepare for the long winter, they must eat and become grossly fat by late fall. In the spring, when they emerge they are thinner, and some have cubs. You don't want to put a fat, well-fed bear in a spring setting.

In this section, you will find patterns for all three bears. Each has been drawn in a walking pose and a standing pose. Look at these patterns closely and you can see how artists can take their knowledge of one species and adapt it to another pose—or even another species. You can reposition any one of the bears with the help of the walking chart and the skeletal drawing also included in this section. Just try it.

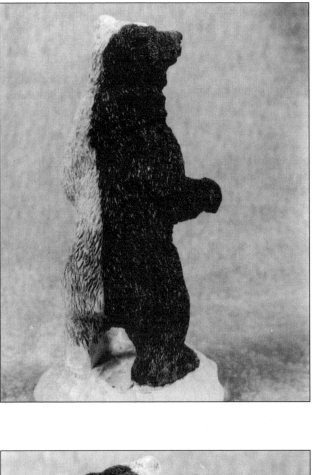

Carving Notes

If you are carving the standing bear, transfer your pattern to a 7" x 3¼" x 3" block of wood with the grain running vertically. The block of wood for the standing polar bear will need to be 7½" x 3¼" x 3".

If you are carving the walking bear, use an 8½" x 4¾" x 2¼" block of wood with the grain running vertically.

If you've altered the pattern, make sure to allow enough wood for shifts in the joints and balance, the curve of the spine, and other alterations.

Eye sockets are at a 65 degree angle from the centerline.

Use Drawing G to measure out the head of your chosen bear.

Use Charts H through K to carve each part of the face.

Use Chart L if you want to add a partial snarl to your bear's facial expression. Notice the lip, which is very flexible, is lifted away from the cuspids so that the teeth are exposed. Move the surface of the teeth below the lip surface so it looks like the teeth are inside the mouth. Woodburn the shape of the teeth. You can carve them further if you'd like by using a series of inverted pyramids (check key).

Hollow out the area behind the shoulder and elbow to show you have allowed for movement.

Notice on Chart N and on the skeleton that there is also a hollow area above the femur. Gouge this area out slightly with a #10 gouge or a Tree Radius Small (¾") bit.

Use Chart M to carve the feet. Remember the grizzly bear has longer claws than the polar or the black bear.

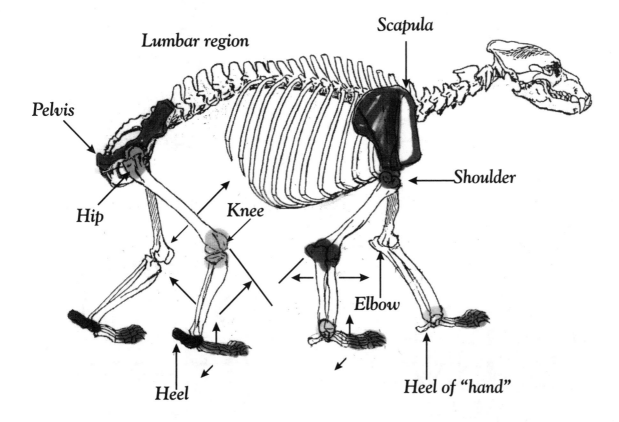

Lumbar region

Scapula

Pelvis

Hip

Knee

Shoulder

Elbow

Heel

Heel of "hand"

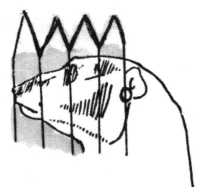

Polar Bear
4 pencil widths long

Polar Bear
3 pencil widths, 4 with ears

Black Bear
4 pencil widths wide, (5 with ears), 5 pencil widths tall

Grizzly Bear
5 pencil widths wide, 5 pencil widths tall

Nose pad is pencil width. Eye socket is pencil width from center line.

Bear Eyes: Carving Tips

1. Draw or V-cut (Or inverted cone)

2. Inverted pyramid (Tapered cone)

3. Undercut (Cylinder)

4. Woodburn

Polar

Black

Grizzly

CHART I

Bear Nose: Carving Tips

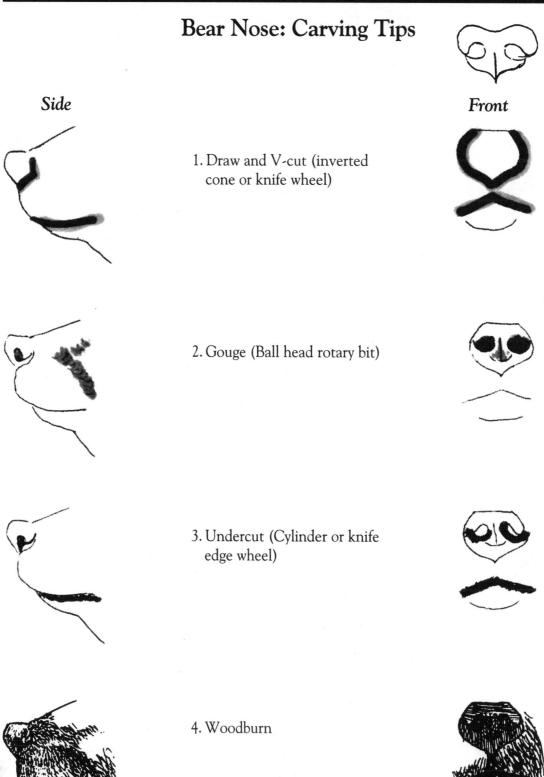

Side

Front

1. Draw and V-cut (inverted cone or knife wheel)

2. Gouge (Ball head rotary bit)

3. Undercut (Cylinder or knife edge wheel)

4. Woodburn

Bear Ears: Carving Tips

1. Draw and trim

3. Hollow out (gouge or a ball bit)

2. V-cut (inverted cone)

4. Woodburn

Bear Face: Surface Texture

CHART L

Note "V shape in nose when snarling

Bear Paw: Carving Tips

Side   *Front*

1. Draw trim

2. V-cut (cone)

3. Shape up and detail as you desire

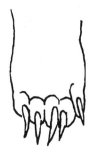

4. Woodburn

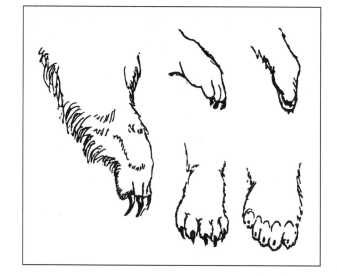

Walking

Polar
Bear
Tracks

Black
Bear
Tracks

Grizzly Bear

Polar Bear

Black Bear

Eyes are halfway between the nose and base of ears

Grizzly Bear Tracks

L.Hind

R.Front

Brown Bear Hair Tract

Right Hind

Polar Bear Hair Tract

Grizzly Hair Tract

Check photos for more information on the flow of the hair.

Black Bear Hair Tract

Walking Polar Bear

Standing Polar Bear

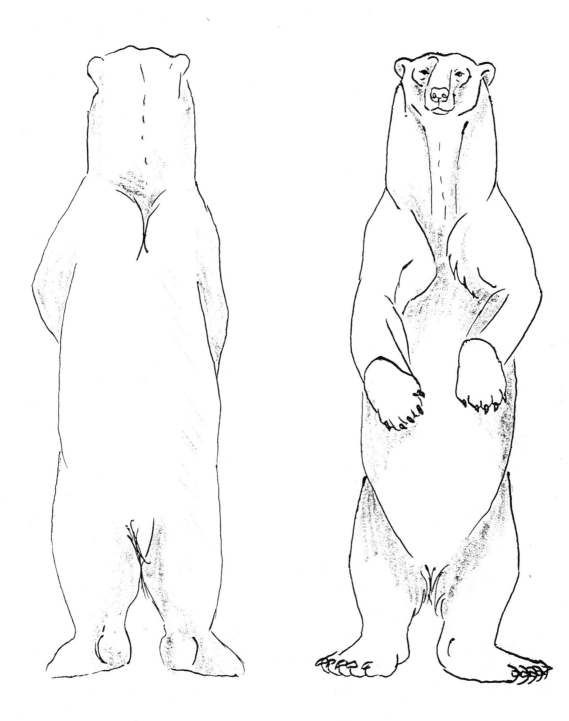

Walking Grizzly Bear

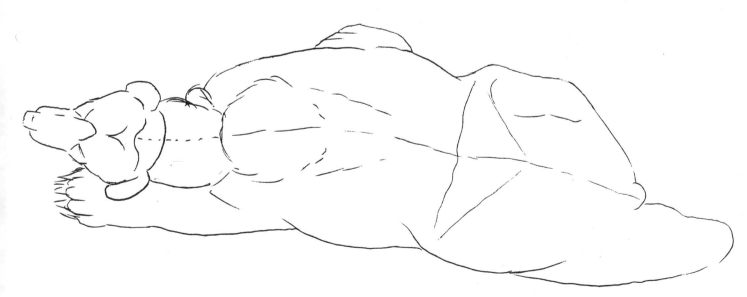

Standing Brown Bear

Standing Black Bear

Walking Black Bear

Bear Cubs

BLACK BEAR CUB

Front View

Top View

Side View

BROWN BEAR CUB

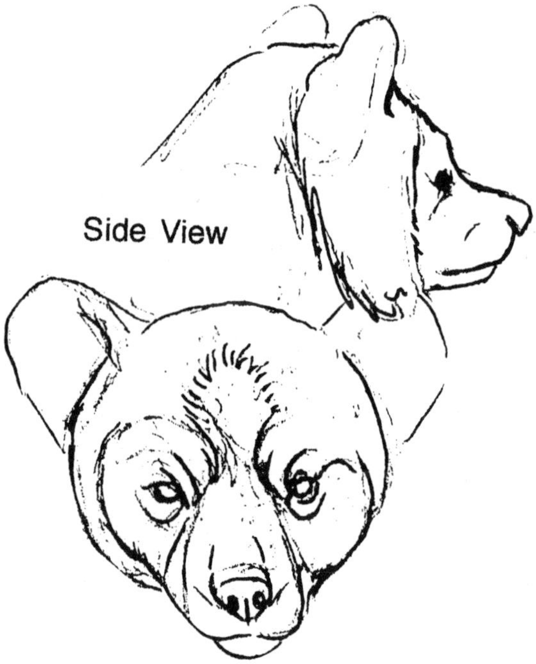

Side View

Front View

POLAR BEAR CUB

Side View

Front View

Note the location of the bear's joints in these different poses.

Bear Teeth

If you decide to open your bear's mouth, you need to know the location and number of the teeth.

Cuspids hook together when the mouth is closed. The lower cuspids are in front of the upper cuspids. When the jaw opens the lower cuspids are exposed. The upper cuspids are only exposed in a snarl or a bite or a yawn. In a snarl, the nose wrinkles up and causes the skin that hangs over the upper teeth to pull up.

There are six incisors between the cuspids (both upper and lower).

Bears are omnivorous, so they also have molars for grinding their food whether it is plant or meat. There is a space behind the cuspids for grabbing and holding on to prey. Bears have 14 molars.

Index

Additional Resources Available

Instructional Video

Sculpturing a Red Fox Out of Wood
by Desiree Hajny

This 83 minute video focuses on creativity, carving, woodburning, and painting. Cost of the video is $30. Available only in North America.

Carving Patterns and Hair Tract Illustrations

Bugling Elk
Fighting Elk
Jumping Deer (Whitetail or Mule Deer)
Running Bison
Standing Bison
Bighorn Sheep
Dahl Sheep
Desert Sheep
Chipmunk
Raccoon
Black Bear
Grizzly Bear
Polar Bear

Cost for each pattern is $1.75 each. Hair tract included.

Send orders to:

Desiree Hajny
1707 S. Shiloh
Wichita, KS 67207

Encyclopedia of Bird Reference Drawings
by David Mohrhardt

"I feel this book will become the one most frequently opened in your studio. You will find it unique in that it offers information not always provided in other reference books". -Bob Guge

This re-issue classic features detailed sketches and wing studies for more than 215 different birds. Includes lots of hard to find information. David is an award winning artist, has been featured at the Leigh Yawkey Woodsom Museum and has a real gift for teaching. We recommend this book as an excellent general reference. Great buy for all carvers, bird lovers and artists.

1-56523-009-4 $14.95

Carving Books by Ivan Whillock

Ivan Whillock is a creative master woodcarver. His books are easy to follow with clear directions and excellent step-by-step photographs and sketches.

Pictorial Relief Carving- projects and patterns
17 projects many photos
Whill2 $9.95

Head Proportions Made Simple
This book will be of real help in understanding what you need to carve faces and figures.
Whill1 $6.00

Carving the Head in Wood- Step-by-step Instruction.
Good clear instructions with over 200 photos cover all aspects from start to finish.
Whill3 $14.95

Carving Characters with Jim Maxwell

New printing of this popular book! Jim has included twelve of his all-time favorite patterns drawn from childhood memories. These projects are designed to be easy to carve whether you are a beginner or advanced carver. These projects feature step-by-step photos and instructions making it easy to quickly understand Jim's techniques and procedures. Want to carve characters? This book takes you from start to finish.

 # Maxwell1   only $6.95

Making Collectible Santas and Christmas Ornaments in Wood.

These 42 easy-to-follow projects will make you very popular this Christmas! Great items for money-making sales as well. This wonderful book presents a variety of projects from traditional to modern, including Santa Clauses and replicas of antique toy ornaments.

Jim and his wife Margie have been making unique carved Santas and wooden Christmas ornaments for over a decade. This new book replaces their earlier book "Carving Christmas Tree Ornaments" and offers eight new, never-before-published patterns for you to make. Highly recommended and a great value.

#Maxwell2   only $6.95

Mammals - An Artistic Approach

Desiree Hajny- to publish first book in Fall 1993.
Nebraska carver Desiree Hajny, well known for her carving seminars and beautiful carved animals will be sharing her knowledge and carving secrets in a new book to be published this fall. Tentatively titled "Mammals: An Artistic Approach" it will be both an excellent reference work on anatomy as well as a complete step-by-step technique book with detailed patterns. This book will start out by teaching you all about mammal anatomy and movement. Then Desiree walks you through some projects step-by-step so you can pick up her tips and techniques in an easy, natural way. Use the patterns to start your own projects then finish it off using Desiree's hair tract burning patterns and painting directions.
Patterns Included: Deer and Fawn, River Otters, Black Bear + more.
Mammals: An Artistic Approach (Hajny 1) $19.95

WOODCARVER'S WORKBOOK

Best woodcarving pattern book I have seen in my 40 years as a carver!
Ed Gallenstein, President
National Woodcarvers Association
Through her articles in Chip Chats-the National Wood Carvers Association magazine- Master artist Mary Duke Guldan has helped thousands of carvers develop their carving skills.
Follow these complete step-by-step instructions and easy to follow patterns-soon you will be creating beautiful hand carved pieces of your own. A special section on painting and finishing your heirloom carving is found in the back of the book.
Look inside and see for yourself why this book is considered a classic by both beginner and veteran carvers.
This excellent woodcarving manual features patterns for : Cougar, Rabbit, Wolf Dogs, Whitetail Deer, Bighorn Sheep,Wild Mustang Horse,Unicorn, Moose
Woodcarvers Workbook (guldan) $14.95

Second Woodcarvers Workbook

All-new patterns, projects and techniques from your favorite carving author. This new book will contain more than just animals.
Partial Listing of Pattern Contents
Texas Longhorn, Cows, Bulls and Farm Animals
Native Indian Chief, Elk, Bears
Second Woodcarvers Workbook Fall 1993 (guldan2) $14.95

Carving Wooden Critters
by Diane Ernst

Curious bunnies, playful puppies- the projects in this book are cute! Delightful patterns at a great price! This inexpensive book features more than a dozen great projects. Easy to follow, clear patterns. Step-by-step beginners' section in front. Great gift and sale items ideas.

(Ernst1) only $6.95

Take a Look at Our Other Fine Woodworking Books

Encyclopedia of Bird Reference Drawings
by David Mohrhardt
"I feel this book will become the one most frequently opened in your studio. You will find it unique in that it offers information not always provided in other reference books". -Bob Guge

This re-issue classic features detailed sketches and wing studies for more than 215 different birds. Includes lots of hard to find information. David is an award winning artist, has been featured at the Leigh Yawkey Woodsom Museum and has a real gift for teaching. We recommend this book as an excellent general reference. Great buy for all carvers, bird lovers and artists.

1-56523-009-4 $14.95

Carving Books
by Ivan Whillock
Ivan Whillock is a creative master woodcarver. His books are easy to follow with clear directions and excellent step-by-step photographs and sketches.

Pictorial Relief Carving- projects and patterns
17 projects many photos
Whill2 $9.95

Head Proportions Made Simple
This book will be of real help in understanding what you need to carve faces and figures.
Whill1 $6.00

Carving the Head in Wood- Step-by-step Instruction.
Good clear instructions with over 200 photos cover all aspects from start to finish.
Whill3 $14.95

Carving Characters with Jim Maxwell
New printing of this popular book! Jim has included twelve of his all-time favorite patterns drawn from childhood memories. These projects are designed to be easy to carve whether you are a beginner or advanced carver. These projects feature step-by-step photos and instructions making it easy to quickly understand Jim's techniques and procedures. Want to carve characters? This book takes you from start to finish.
 # Maxwell1   only $6.95

Making Collectible Santas and Christmas Ornaments in Wood.
These 42 easy-to-follow projects will make you very popular this Christmas! Great items for money-making sales as well. This wonderful book presents a variety of projects from traditional to modern, including Santa Clauses and replicas of antique toy ornaments.
Jim and his wife Margie have been making unique carved Santas and wooden Christmas ornaments for over a decade. This new book replaces their earlier book "Carving Christmas Tree Ornaments" and offers eight new, never-before-published patterns for you to make. Highly recommended and a great value.
#Maxwell2   only $6.95

Mammals - An Artistic Approach
Desiree Hajny- to publish first book in Fall 1993.
Nebraska carver Desiree Hajny, well known for her carving seminars and beautiful carved animals will be sharing her knowledge and carving secrets in a new book to be published this fall. Tentatively titled "Mammals: An Artistic Approach" it will be both an excellent reference work on anatomy as well as a complete step-by-step technique book with detailed patterns. This book will start out by teaching you all about mammal anatomy and movement. Then Desiree walks you through some projects step-by-step so you can pick up her tips and techniques in an easy, natural way. Use the patterns to start your own projects then finish it off using Desiree's hair tract burning patterns and painting directions.
Patterns Included: Deer and Fawn, River Otters, Black Bear + more.
Mammals: An Artistic Approach (Hajny 1) $19.95

WOODCARVER'S WORKBOOK
Best woodcarving pattern book I have seen in my 40 years as a carver!
Ed Gallenstein, President
National Woodcarvers Association
Through her articles in Chip Chats- the National Wood Carvers Association magazine- Master artist Mary Duke Guldan has helped thousands of carvers develop their carving skills.
Follow these complete step-by-step instructions and easy to follow patterns-soon you will be creating beautiful hand carved pieces of your own. A special section on painting and finishing your heirloom carving is found in the back of the book.
Look inside and see for yourself why this book is considered a classic by both beginner and veteran carvers.
This excellent woodcarving manual features patterns for : Cougar, Rabbit, Wolf Dogs, Whitetail Deer, Bighorn Sheep,Wild Mustang Horse,Unicorn, Moose
Woodcarvers Workbook (guldan) $14.95

Second Woodcarvers Workbook
All-new patterns, projects and techniques from your favorite carving author. This new book will contain more than just animals.
Partial Listing of Pattern Contents
Texas Longhorn, Cows, Bulls and Farm Animals
Native Indian Chief, Elk, Bears
Second Woodcarvers Workbook Fall 1993 (guldan2) $14.95

Carving Wooden Critters
by Diane Ernst
Curious bunnies, playful puppies- the projects in this book are cute! Delightful patterns at a great price! This inexpensive book features more than a dozen great projects. Easy to follow, clear patterns. Step-by-step beginners' section in front. Great gift and sale items ideas.
(Ernst1) only $6.95

Take a Look at Our Other Fine Woodworking Books

Woodcarving Books by George Lehman

Learn new techniques as you carve these projects designed by professional artists and carver George Lehman. These best-selling books by a master carver are invaluable reference books, PLUS each book contains over 20 ready-to-use patterns.

Book One - **Carving Realistic Game and Songbirds - Patterns and instructions**

Enthusiastically received by carvers across the US and Canada. George pays particular attention to the needs of beginning carvers in this volume. 20 patterns, over 70 photos, sketches and reference drawing.

ISBN# 1-56523-004-3   96 pages, spiral bound, 14 x 11 inches, includes index, resources $19.95

Book Two - **Realism in Wood - 22 projects, detailed patterns and instructions**

This volume features a selection of patterns for shorebirds and birds of prey in addition to all-new duck and songbird patterns. Special sections on adding detail, burning.

ISBN# 1-56523-005-1,   112 pages, spiral bound, 14 x 11 inches, includes index, resources $19.95

Book Three - **Nature in Wood - patterns for carving 21 smaller birds and 8 wild animals**

Focuses on songbirds and small game birds. Numerous tips and techniques throughout including instruction on necessary skills for creating downy feather details and realistic wings. Wonderful section on wild animal carvings with measured patterns.

ISBN #1-56523-006-X   128 pages, soft bound, 11 x 8.5 inches, includes index, resources $16.95

Book Four - **Carving Wildlife in Wood- 20 Exciting Projects**

Here is George's newest book for decorative woodcarvers with never-before-published patterns. Tremendously detailed, these patterns appeal to carvers at all skill levels. Patterns for birds of prey, ducks, wild turkey, shorebirds and more! Great addition to any carvers library - will be used again and again.

ISBN #1-56523-007-8   96 pages, spiral-bound, 14 x 11 inches, includes index, resources $19.95

Easy to Make Wooden Inlay Projects: Intarsia   *by Judy Gale Roberts*

Intarsia is a method of making picture mosaics in wood, using a combination of wood grains and colors. The techniques and step-by-step instructions in this book will have you completing your own beautiful pieces in short order. Written by acknowledged expert Judy Gale Roberts, who has her own studio and publishes the Intarsia Times newsletter, produces videos, gives seminars and writes articles on the Intarsia method. Each project is featured in full color and this well written, heavily illustrated features over 100 photographs and includes index and directory of suppliers

ISBN# 56523-023-X   250 pages, soft cover, 8.5 x 11 inches $19.95

Two more great scroll saw books by Judy Gale Roberts! Scroll Saw Fretwork Patterns

Especially designed for the scroll saw enthusiast who wishes to excel, the 'fine line design' method helps you to control drift error found with thick line patterns. Each book features great designs, expert tips, and patterns on oversized (up to 11" x 17"!) sheets in a special "lay flat" spiral binding. Choose the original Design Book 1 with animal and fun designs, or Design Book Two featuring "Western- Southwestern" designs.

Scroll Saw Fretwork Pattern, Design Book One "The Original" $14.95

Scroll Saw Fretwork Patterns, Design Book Two "Western-Southwestern" $16.95

Scroll Saw Woodcrafting Magic! Complete Pattern and How-to Manual   *by Joanne Lockwood*

Includes complete patterns drawn to scale. You will be amazed at how easy it is to make these beautiful projects when you follow Joanne's helpful tips and work from these clear, precise patterns. Never-before-published patterns for original and creative toys, jewelry, and gifts. Never used a scroll saw? The tutorials in this book will get you started quickly. Experienced scroll-sawers will delight in these all-new, unique projects, perfect for craft sales and gift-giving. Written by Joanne Lockwood, owner of Three Bears Studio in California and the president of the Sacramento Area Woodworkers; she is frequently featured in national woodwork and craft magazines.

ISBN# 1-56523-024-8   180 pages, soft cover, 8.5 x 11 inches $14.95

Making Signs in Wood with Your Router   *by Paul Merrills*

If you own a router, you can produce beautiful personalized signs and designs easily and inexpensively. This is the complete manual for beginners and professionals. Features over 100 clear photos, easy-to-follow instructions, ready-to-use designs, and six complete sign making alphabets. Techniques range from small nameplates to world-class showpieces trimmed with gold leaf.

ISBN# 56523-026-4 250 pages, 8.5 x 11 inches; includes index and suppliers directory $19.95

- -

To order: If you can't find these at your favorite bookseller you may order direct from the publisher
at the prices listed above plus $2.00 per book shipping.
Send check or money order to:

Fox Chapel Publishing
Box 7948D
Lancaster, Pennsylvania , 17604